PIANO / VOCAL / GUITAR

THE Natalie Grant COLLECTION

ISBN 978-1-4234-9018-0

7777 W. BLUEMOUND RD. P.O. BOX 13819 MILWAUKEE, WI 53213

Visit Hal Leonard Online at
www.halleonard.com

ALWAYS BE YOUR BABY

Words and Music by NATALIE GRANT,
STEPHANIE LEWIS and GEORGE TEREN III

Gently

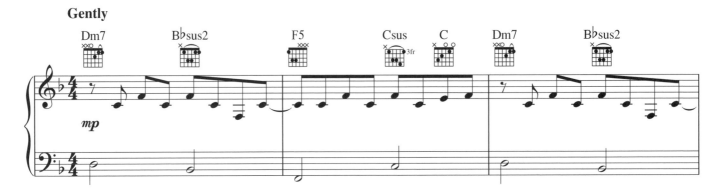

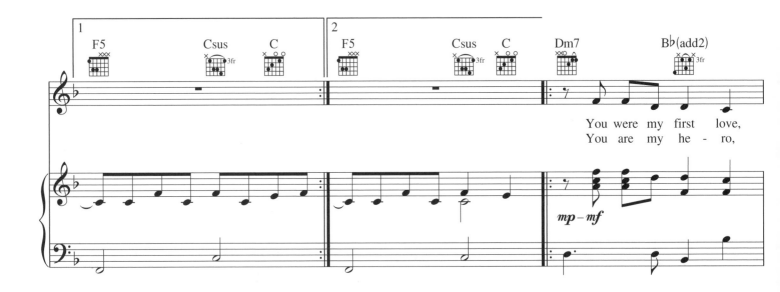

You were my first love,
You are my he - ro,

al - ways there for me.
and that will nev - er change.

You taught me how to walk and
You still can dry my tears with

how to dream. __
just a smile, __

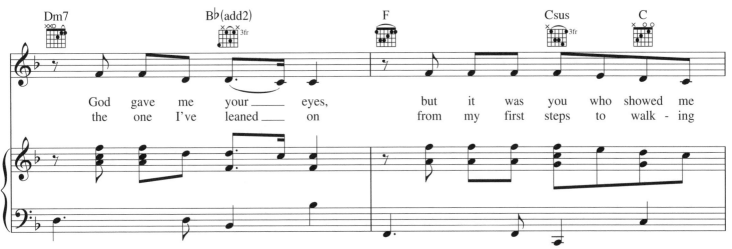

God gave me your ____ eyes,   but it was you who showed me
the one I've leaned ____ on   from my first steps to walk - ing

how to see.   Now   I ____ can
down the aisle.   Now   there's _ an - oth - er

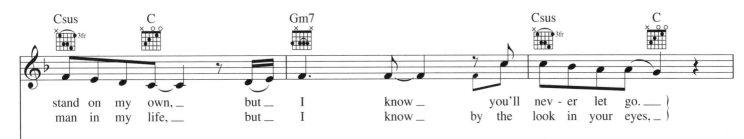

stand on my own, _   but _ I   know _ you'll nev - er let go. __ }
man in my life, __   but _ I   know _ by the look in your eyes, _ }

I'll al - ways be your ba - by, ___   no mat - ter how the years __

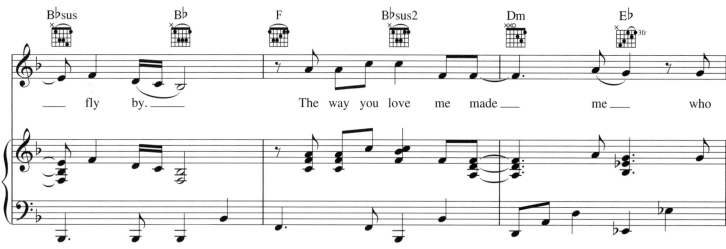

fly by. The way you love me made me who

I am in this world. I'm a wom-an now, not a lit-

-tle girl. Wher-ev-er this life takes me,

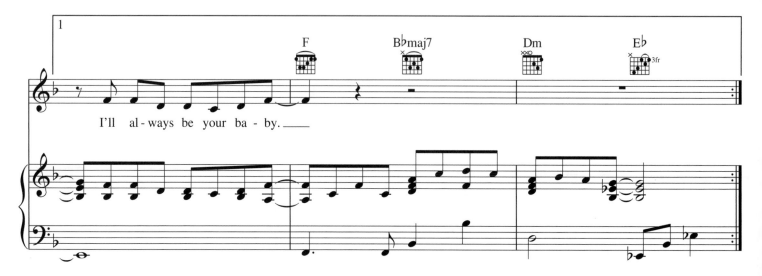

I'll al-ways be your ba-by.

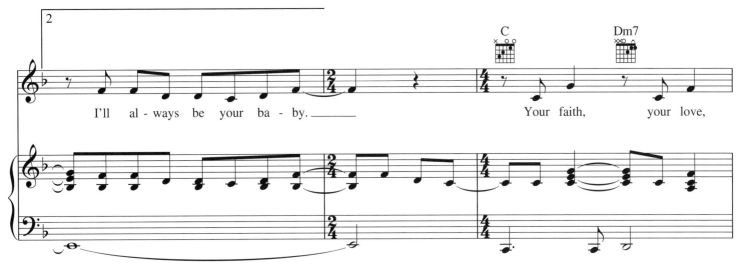

I'll al - ways be your ba - by. _____ Your faith, your love,

and all that you be - lieve have come ____ to be ____ the strong - est part of me.

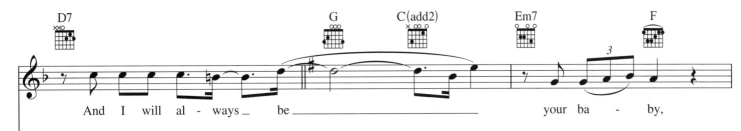

And I will al - ways ___ be _____ your ba - by,

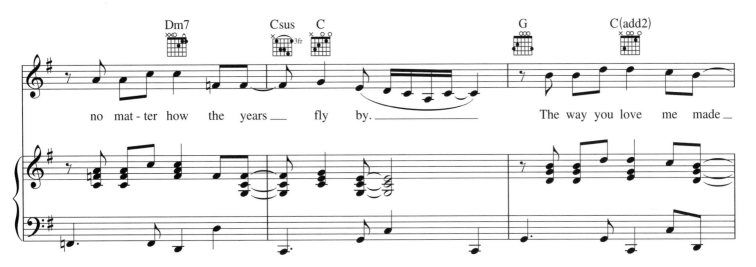

no mat - ter how the years ___ fly by. _____ The way you love me made ___

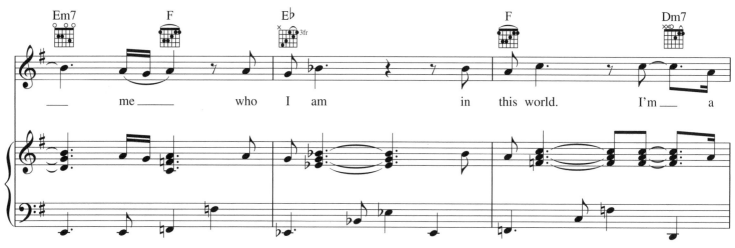

me ___ who I am ___ in this world. I'm ___ a

wom - an now, ___ not a lit - tle girl. ___ Wher - ev - er this life takes ___

___ me, ___ I'll al - ways be your ba - by, ___ al - ways

be your ba - by girl.

HELD

Words and Music by
CHRISTA WELLS

Slow four, with emotion

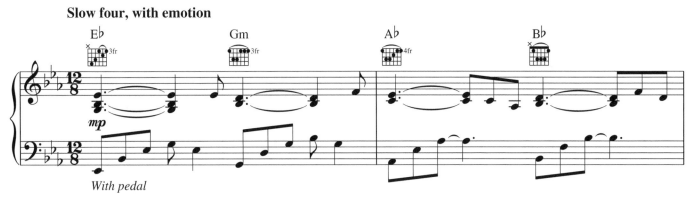

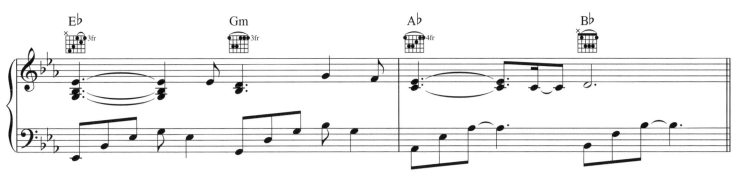

Two months is _____ too lit - tle. They let him go; _____ they had no _____

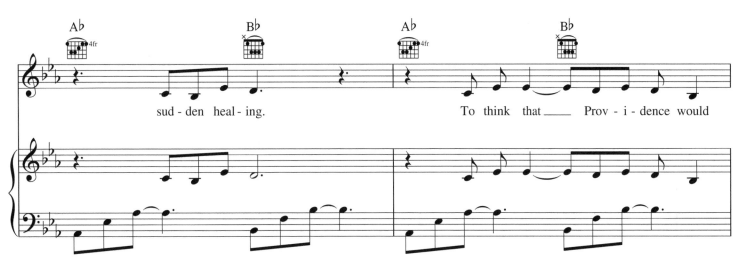

sud - den heal - ing. To think that _____ Prov - i - dence would

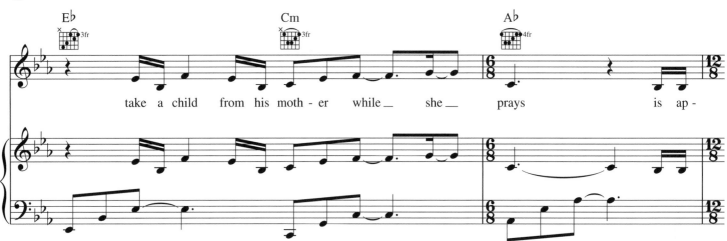

take a child from his moth - er while __ she __ prays is ap -

pall - ing. _____ Who told us _____ we'd be res - cued?

What has changed, and _____ why should we be __ saved _____ from night - mares? ___

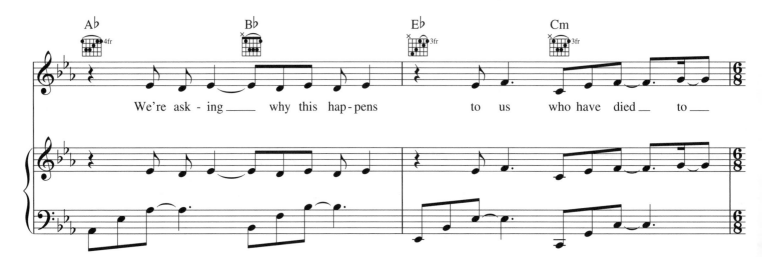

We're ask - ing _____ why this hap - pens to us who have died __ to __

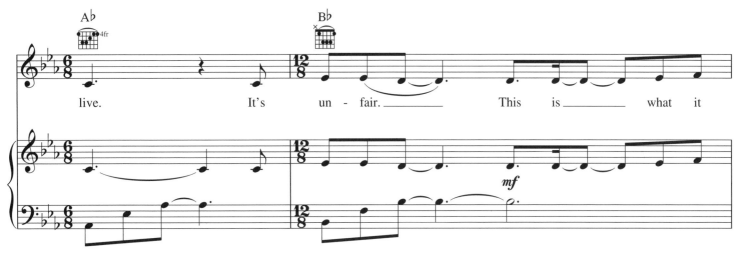

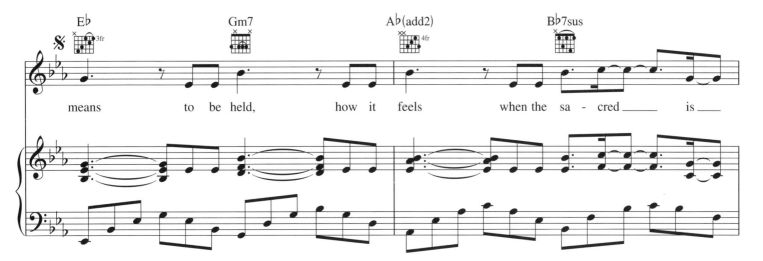

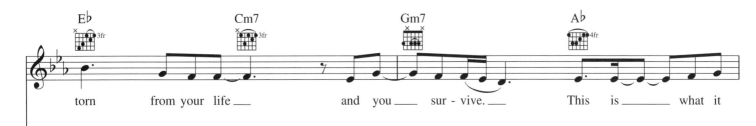

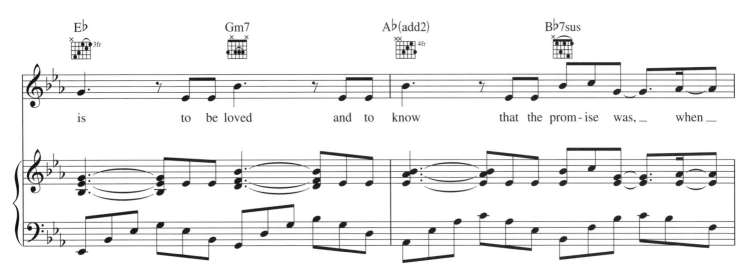

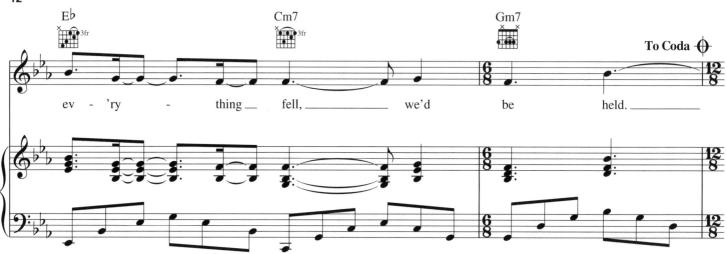

ev - 'ry - thing __ fell, _____ we'd be held. _____

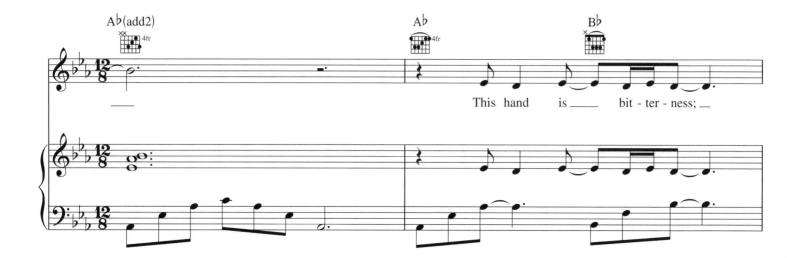

__ This hand is __ bit - ter - ness; __

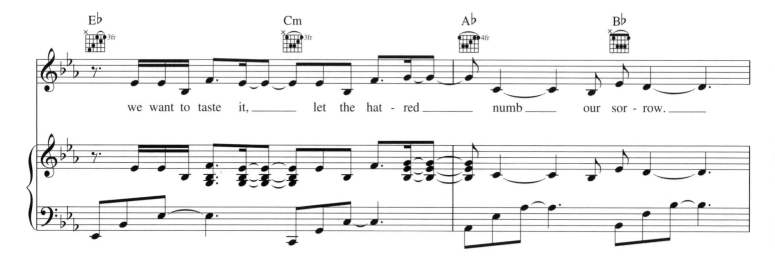

we want to taste it, __ let the hat - red __ numb __ our sor - row. __

The wise hand __ o - pens slow - ly to lil - ies of the val - ley

D.S. al Coda

and _____ to - mor - row. _____ This is _____ what it

CODA

___ If hope is born of ___ suf - fer - ing, ___

mp *mf*

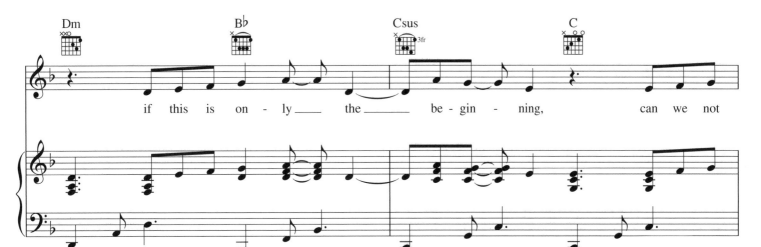

if this is on - ly ___ the ___ be - gin - ning, can we not

wait for one ___ hour, watch - ing for our _____ Sav -

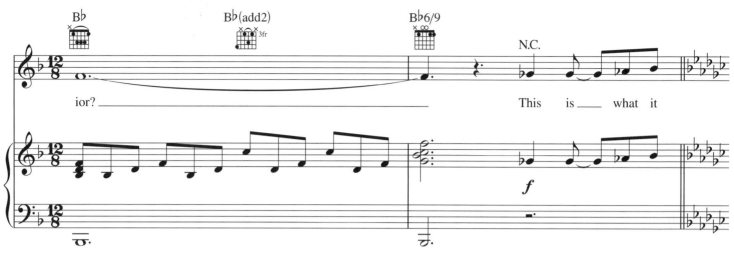

ior? _____ This is ___ what it

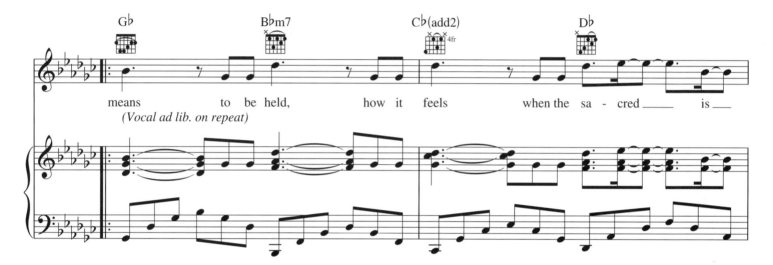

means ___ to be held, how it feels ___ when the sa-cred ___ is ___
(Vocal ad lib. on repeat)

torn ___ from your life ___ and you ___ sur-vive. ___ This is _____ what it

is ___ to be loved ___ and to know ___ that the prom-ise was, ___ when ___

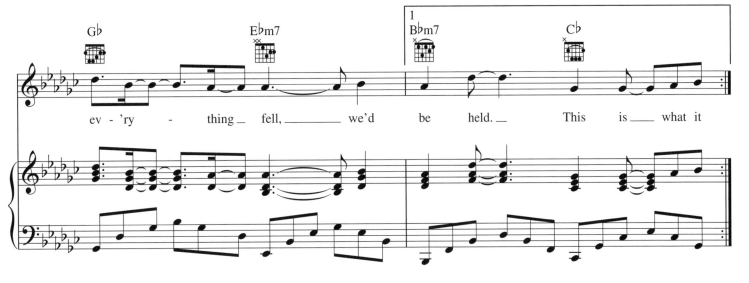

ev - 'ry - thing _ fell, _____ we'd be held. _ This is _ what it

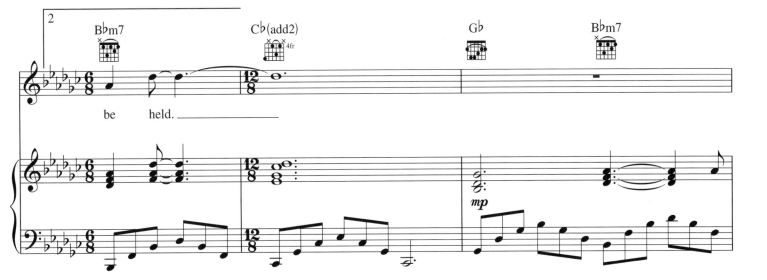

be held. _____

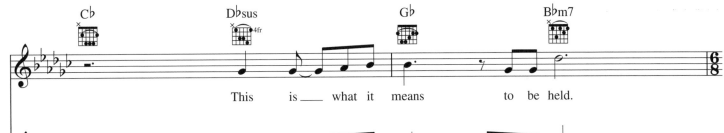

This is _ what it means to be held.

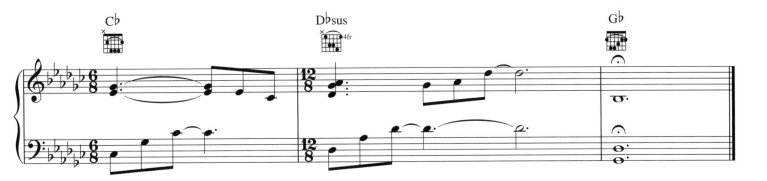

BREATHE ON ME

Words and Music by
NATALIE GRANT

Gentle Ballad

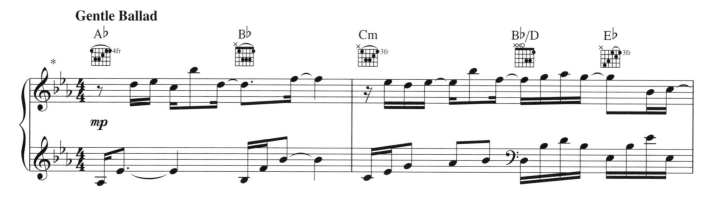

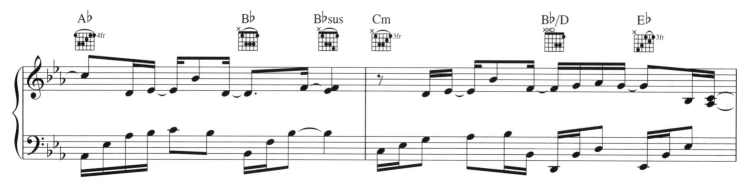

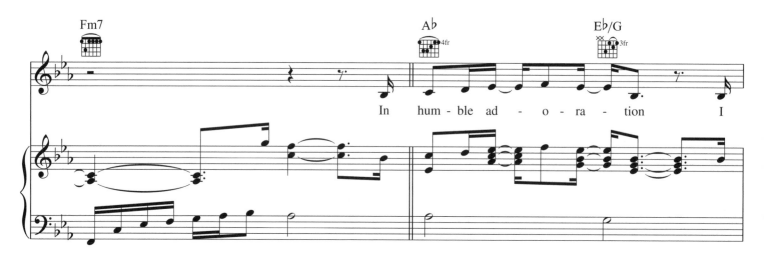

In hum - ble ad - o - ra - tion I

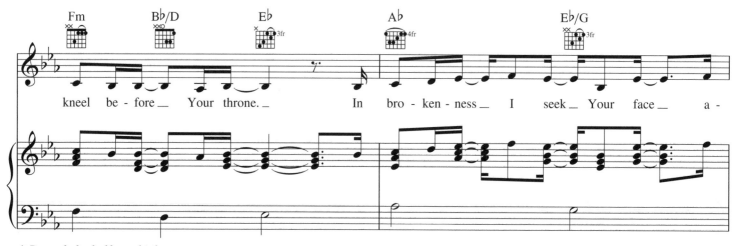

kneel be - fore __ Your throne. __ In bro - ken - ness __ I seek __ Your face __ a -

* *Recorded a half step higher.*

lone.   A - bove You there's _ no oth - er   who's

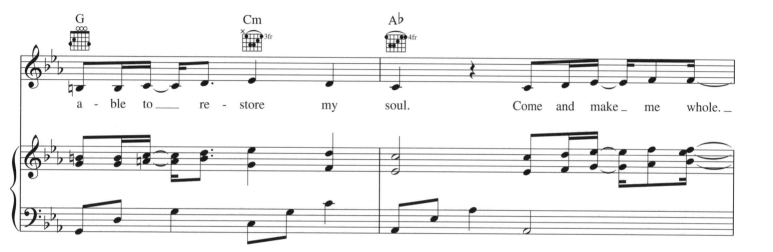

a - ble to __ re - store my soul.   Come and make _ me whole. __

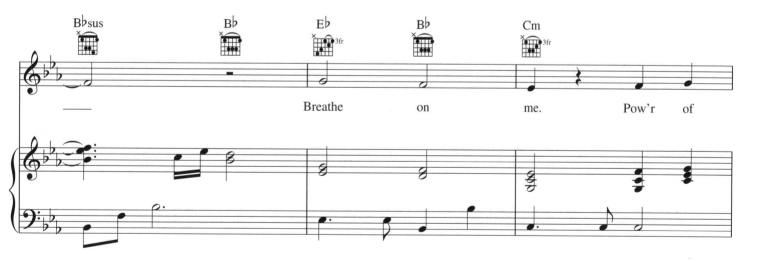

__   Breathe   on   me.   Pow'r of

God, come in ___ and change ___ me.   You are all ___ I need. __

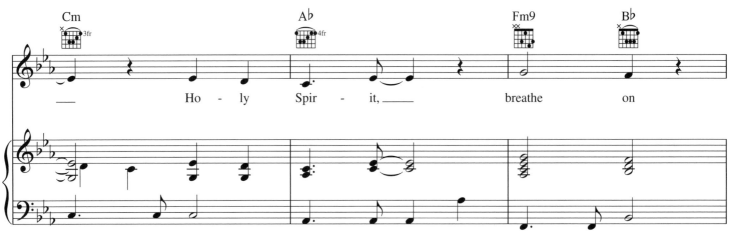

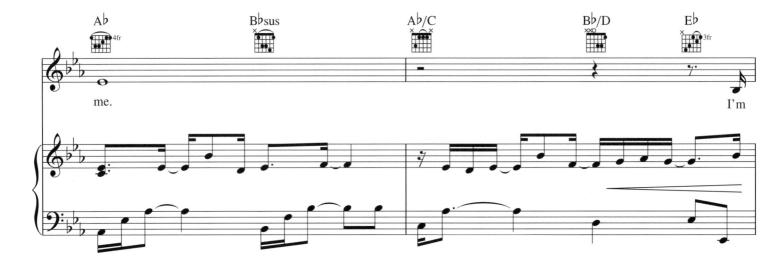

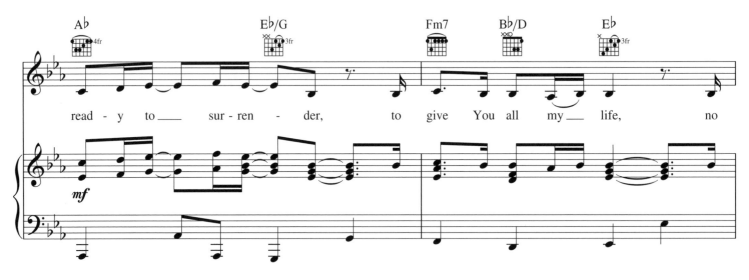

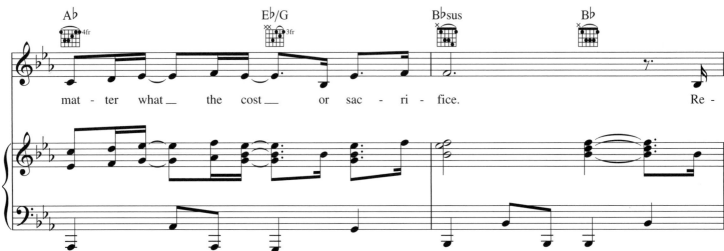

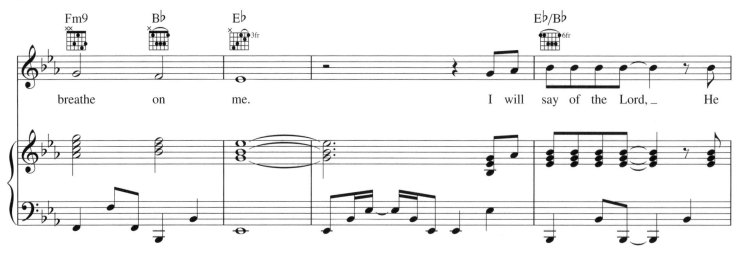

breathe on me. I will say of the Lord, __ He

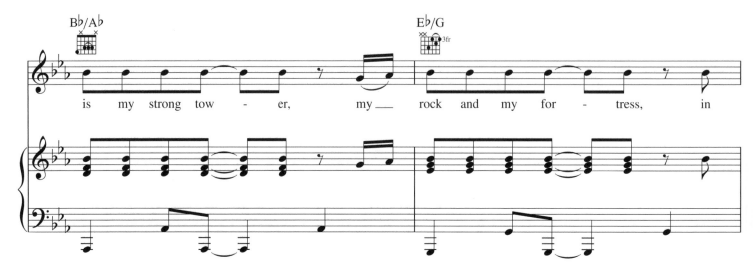

is my strong tow - er, my __ rock and my for - tress, in

whom I trust. In _____ times of the storm _ and in trib - u - la - tion,

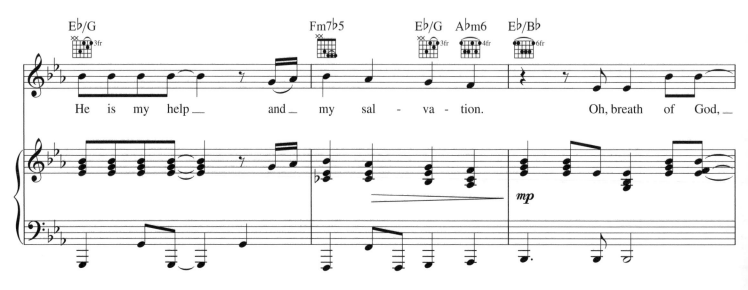

He is my help __ and _ my sal - va - tion. Oh, breath of God, __

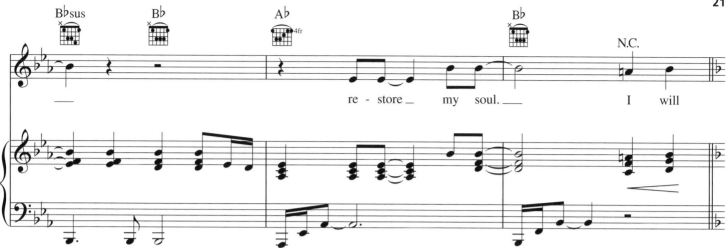

re - store __ my soul. __ I will

say of the Lord, __ He is my strong tow - er, my __

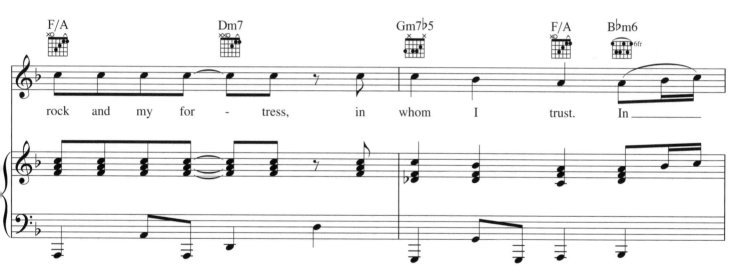

rock and my for - tress, in whom I trust. In __

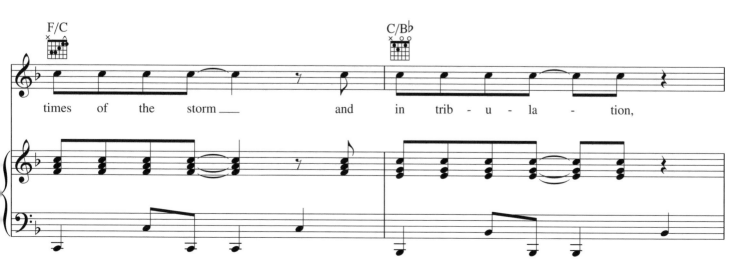

times of the storm __ and in trib - u - la - tion,

He is my help __ and __ my sal - va - tion. Breath of God, __

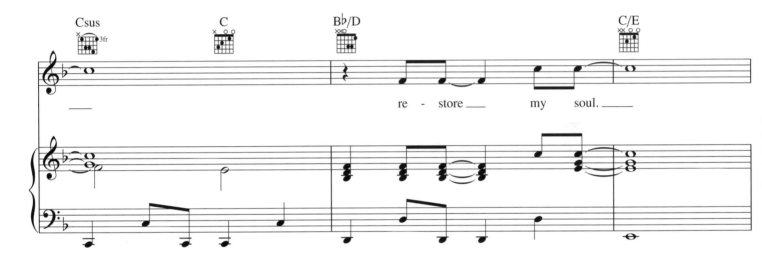

__ re - store __ my soul. __

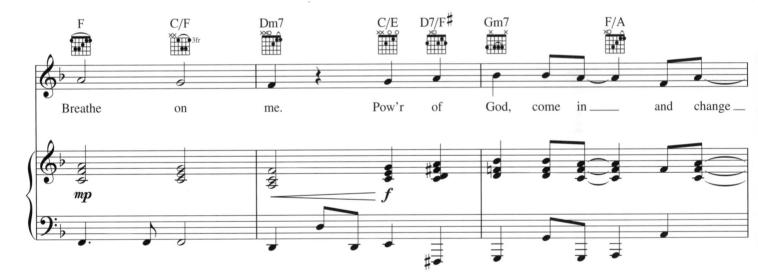

Breathe on me. Pow'r of God, come in __ and change __

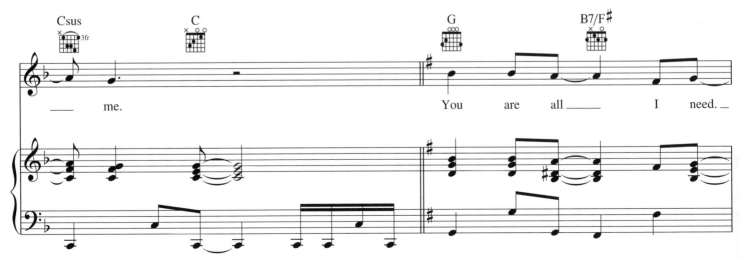

__ me. You are all __ I need. __

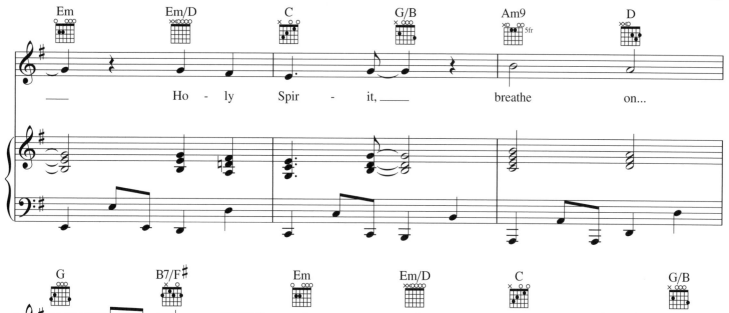

Ho - ly Spir - it, ____ breathe on...

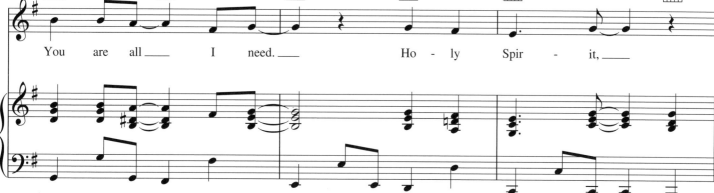

You are all ___ I need. ___ Ho - ly Spir - it, ___

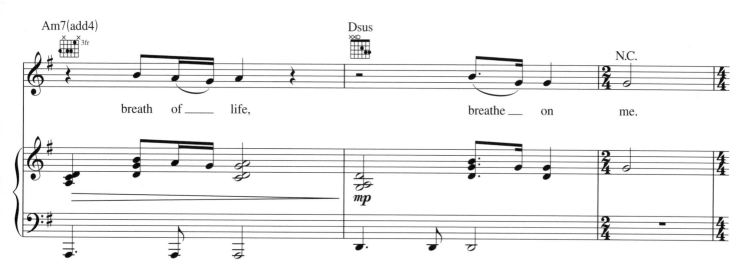

breath of ___ life, breathe ___ on me.

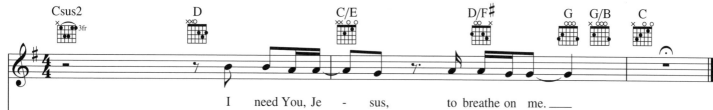

I need You, Je - sus, to breathe on me. ___

I DESIRE

Words and Music by NATALIE GRANT,
BERNIE HERMS and CINDY MORGAN

Here in this world that You've de-signed, from the

roll-ing plains to the o-ceans deep and wide, where are the words

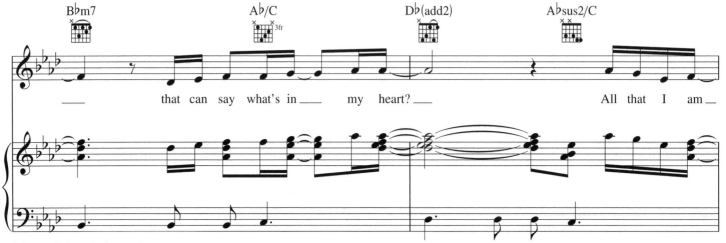

that can say what's in my heart? All that I am

* Recorded a whole step lower.

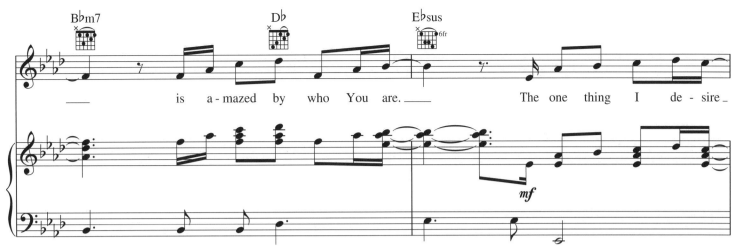

is a-mazed by who You are. ___ The one thing I de-sire ___

___ is just to know ___ You more, ___ to live ___ a life ___

___ that moves ___ and breathes ___ and loves ___ to bring You joy. ___ So fill me with ___ a fire ___

___ that burns a-way ___ my doubts ___ and all my fears, ___ in -

26

to a place ___ where You are all ___ I hear. ___ It's the one thing I de-

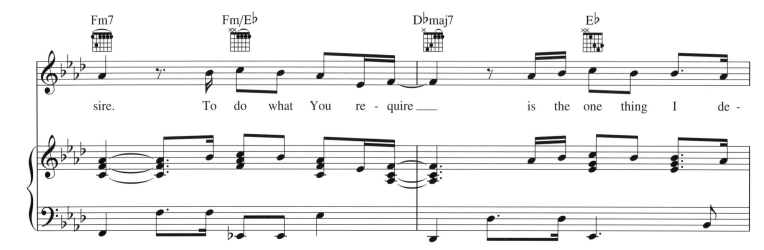

sire. To do what You re-quire ___ is the one thing I de-

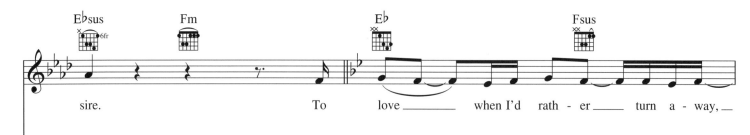

sire. To love ___ when I'd rath-er ___ turn a-way, ___

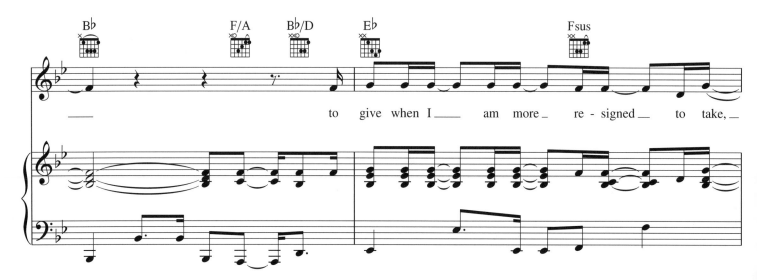

___ to give when I ___ am more ___ re-signed ___ to take, ___

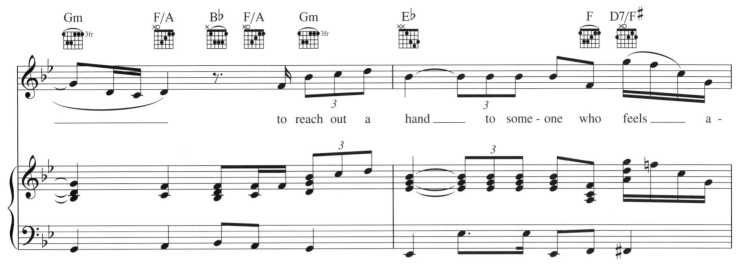

to reach out a hand _____ to some - one who feels _____ a-

lone, _____ the way You reached for me _____ when there seemed to be _____ no

hope. The one thing I de - sire _____ is just to know _ You

more, _____ to live _ a life _____ that moves _ and breathes _ and loves _ to bring _

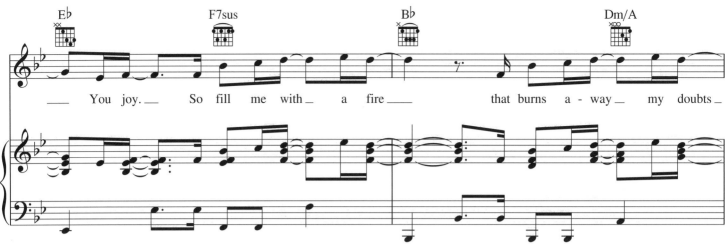

You joy. __ So fill me with __ a fire ___ that burns a-way __ my doubts __

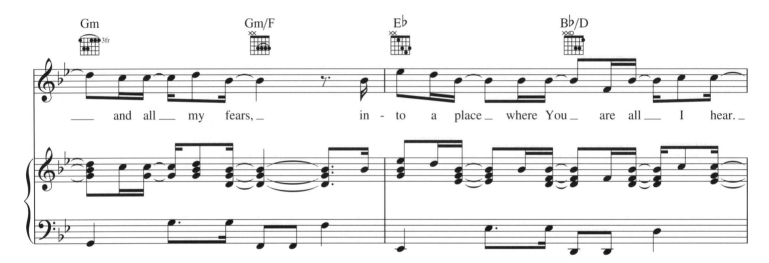

__ and all __ my fears, __ in-to a place __ where You __ are all __ I hear. __

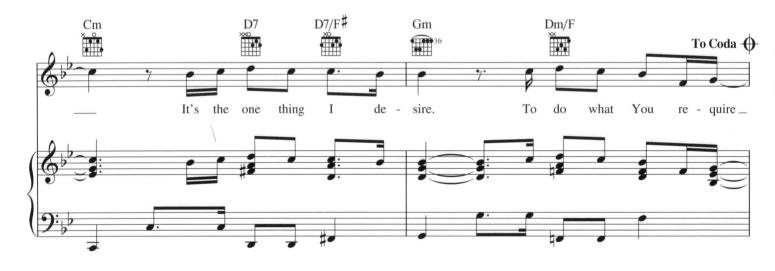

To Coda ⊕

__ It's the one thing I de-sire. To do what You re-quire __

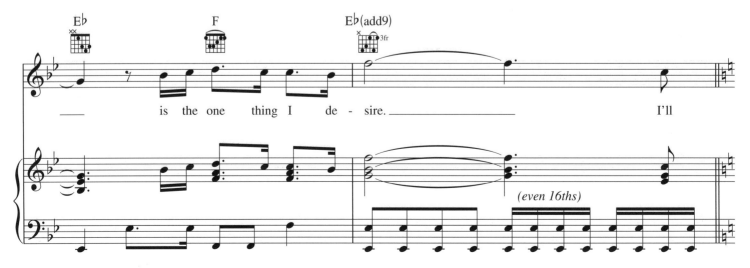

__ is the one thing I de-sire. _____ I'll

(even 16ths)

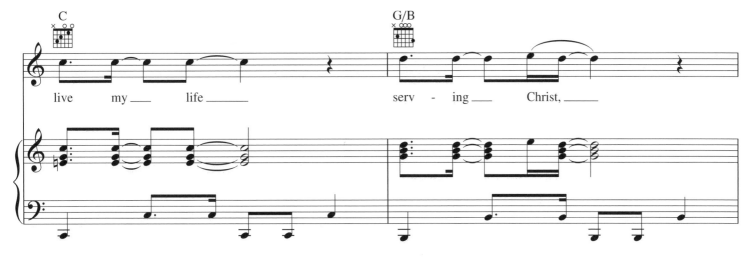

live my ___ life ___ serv - ing ___ Christ, ___

of - fer - ing a sac - ri - fice ___ of ___ praise. ___

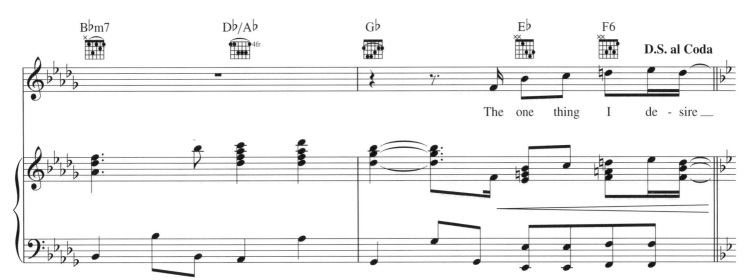

D.S. al Coda

The one thing I de - sire ___

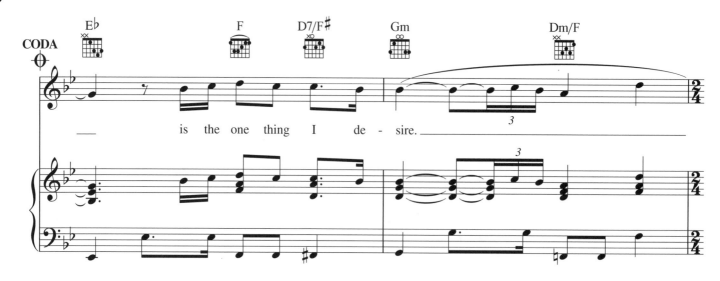

CODA

is the one thing I de - sire.

It's the one thing, ___ is to know ___

___ You. I ___ wan - na know You, Je - sus. You're the

one thing I, ___ I ___ de - sire.

I LOVE TO PRAISE

Words and Music by
NATALIE GRANT

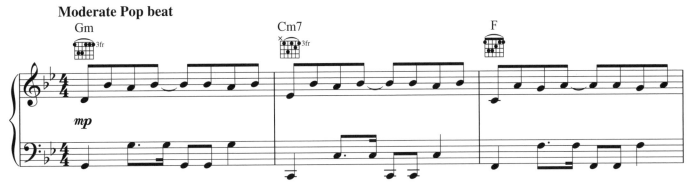

so I can come ___ in spir-it and ___ in truth. _____ To

wor-ship You, ___ that's what ___ I long ___ to _____ do. 'Cause I love to praise, ___

___ I love to lift ___ Your ho-ly name ___ from the

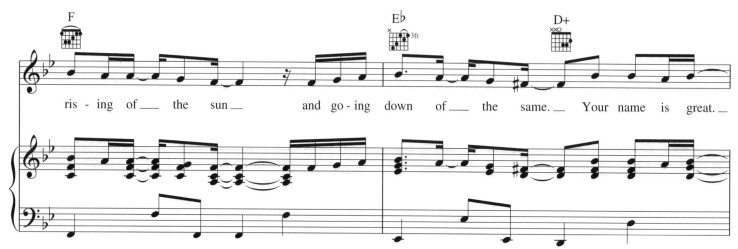

ris-ing of ___ the sun ___ and go-ing down of ___ the same. ___ Your name is great. ___

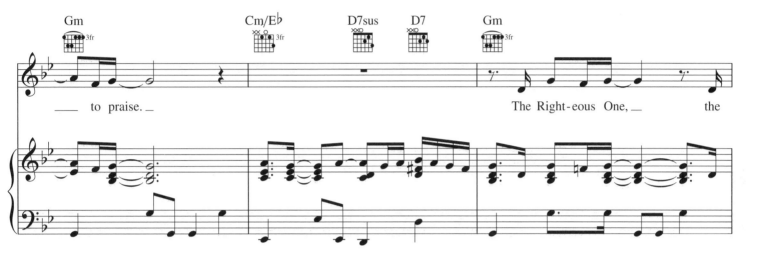

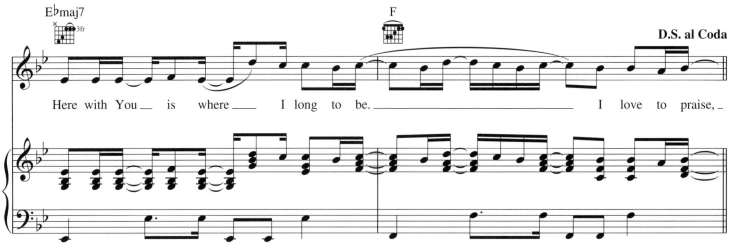

Here with You __ is where __ I long to be. _____ I love to praise, __

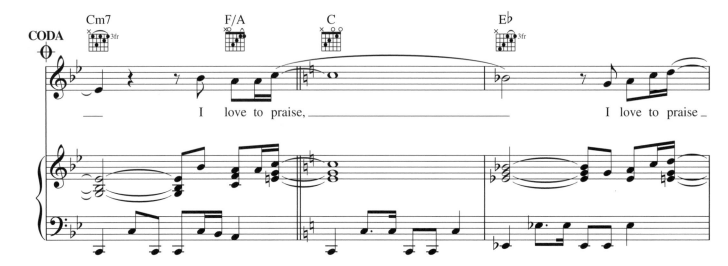

__ I love to praise, _____ I love to praise __

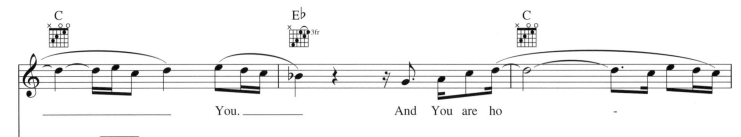

_____ You. _____ And You are ho -

ly. My lips shall al - ways speak __ Your praise. __

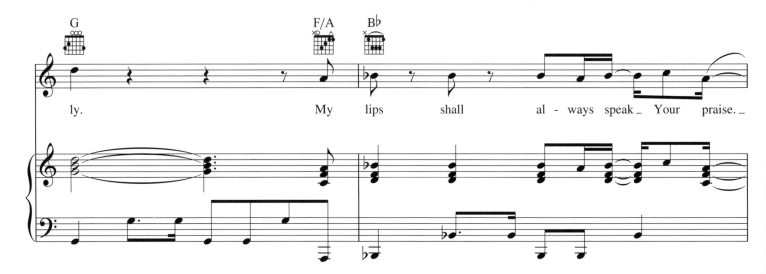

And You __ are wor - thy, __ wor - thy. __ For -

ev - er I __ will al - ways sing __ Your praise.   I love to praise, __   I love to lift __

(Lead vocal ad lib. to end)

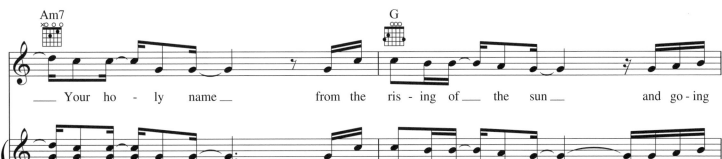

__ Your ho - ly name __   from the ris - ing of __ the sun __   and go - ing

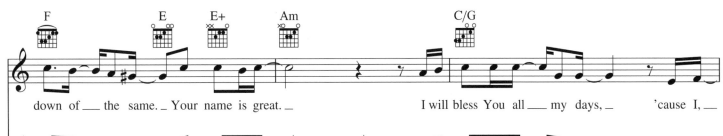

down of __ the same. __ Your name is great. __   I will bless You all __ my days, __   'cause I, __

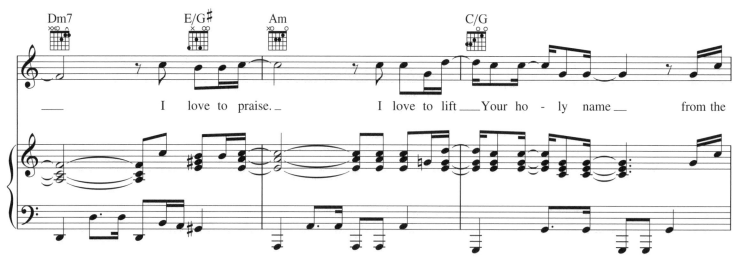

lips shall al - ways speak __ Your praise. __ You are

wor - thy. For - ev - er I __ will al - ways sing __ Your praise.

I WILL BE

Words and Music by NATALIE GRANT,
BERNIE HERMS and PAUL FIELD

hand_ of heav - en a - bove.__ I will be a mir - ror that_ re - flects_

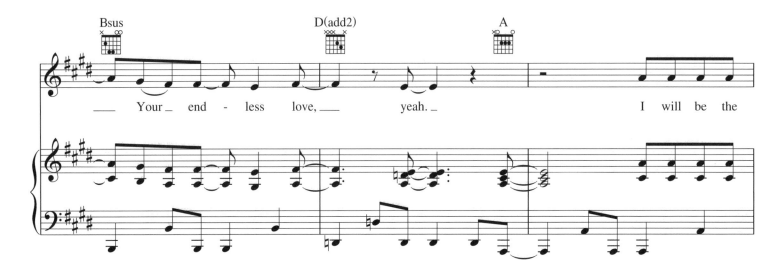

__ Your_ end - less love,__ yeah. _ I will be the

hope_ a - mong_ the hope - less. Where there is con - flict, I__ will be peace.__

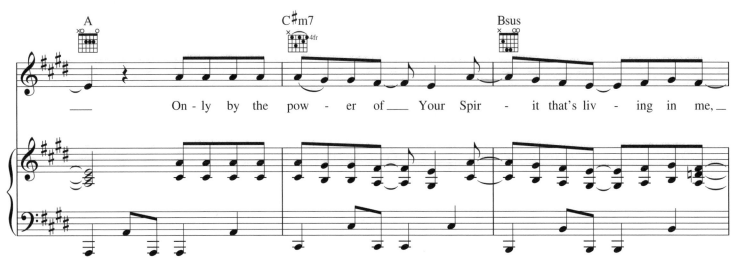

__ On - ly by the pow - er of__ Your Spir - it that's liv - ing in me,__

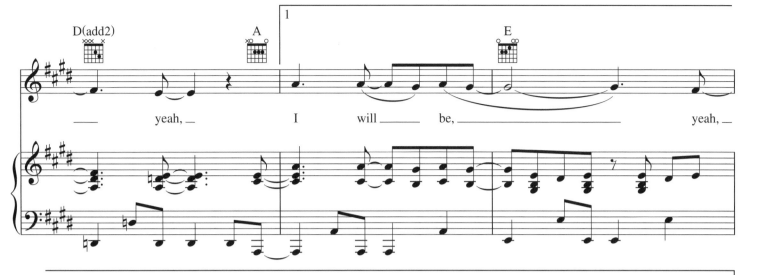

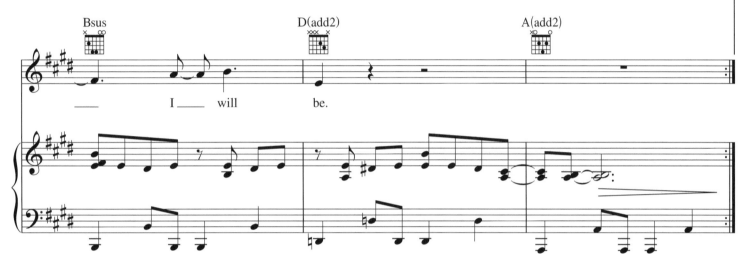

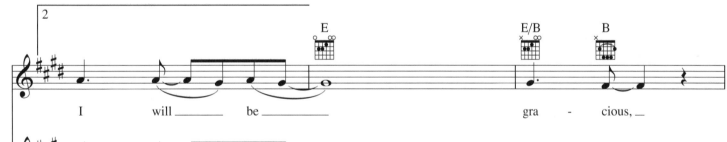

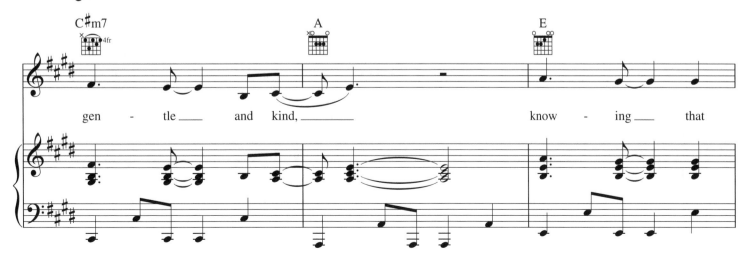

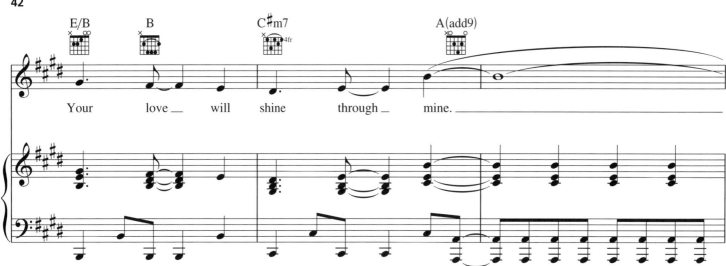

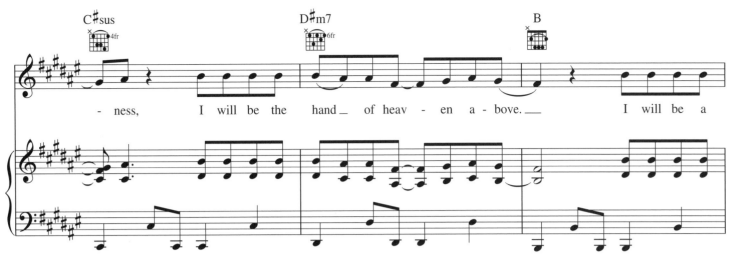

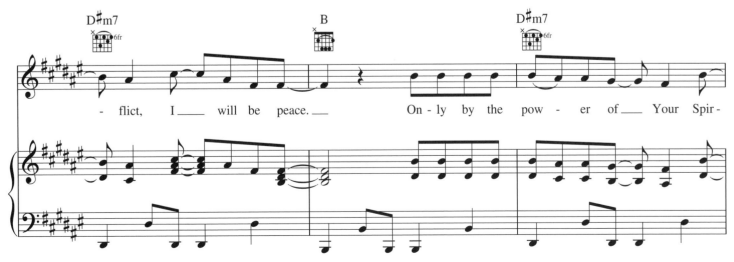

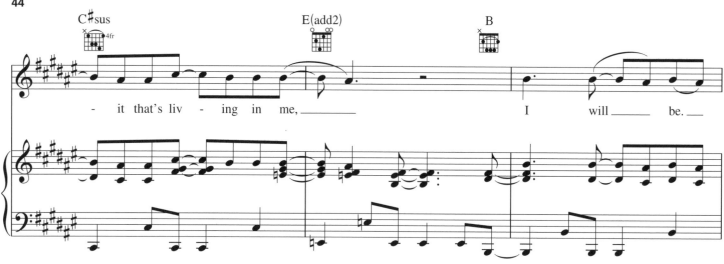

I WILL NOT BE MOVED

Words and Music by
NATALIE GRANT

Driving Rock beat

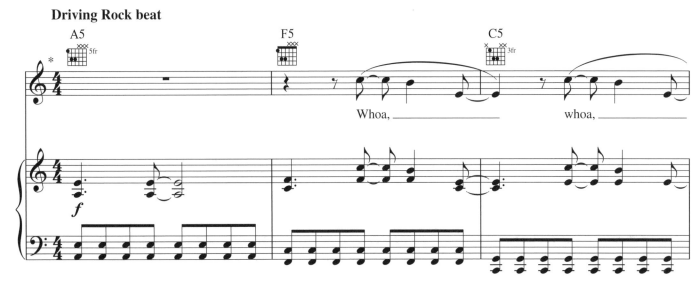

Whoa, _____ whoa, _____

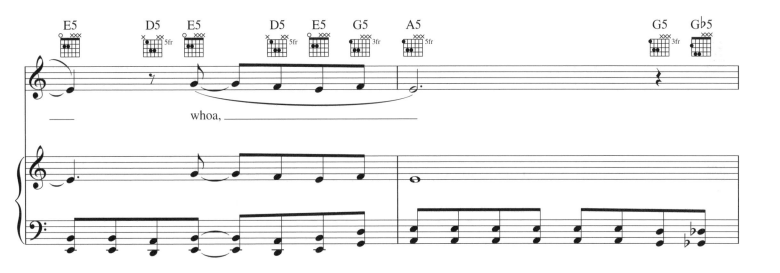

_____ whoa, _____

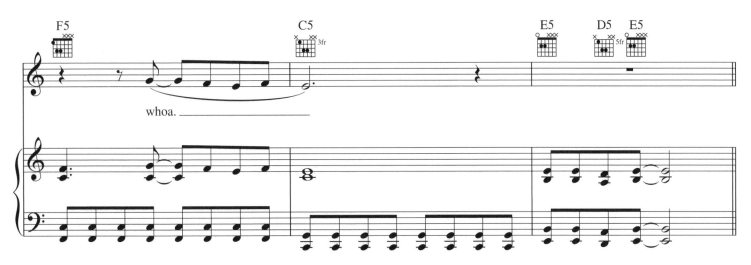

whoa. _____

* *Recorded a half step lower.*

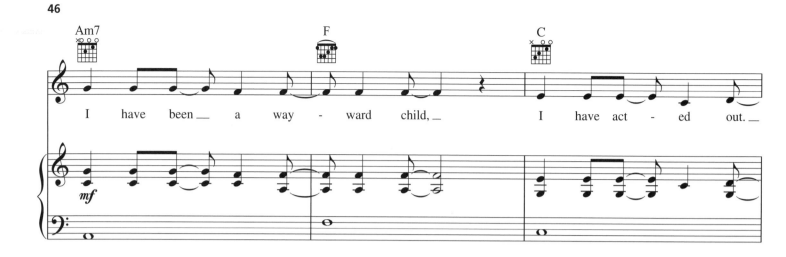

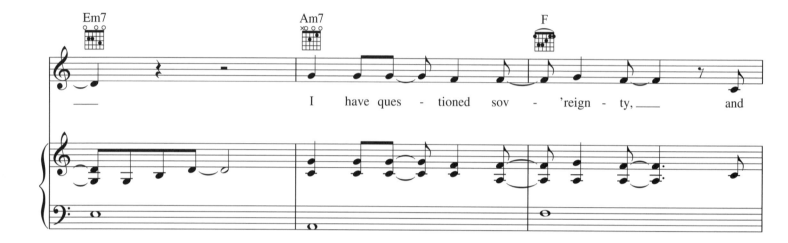

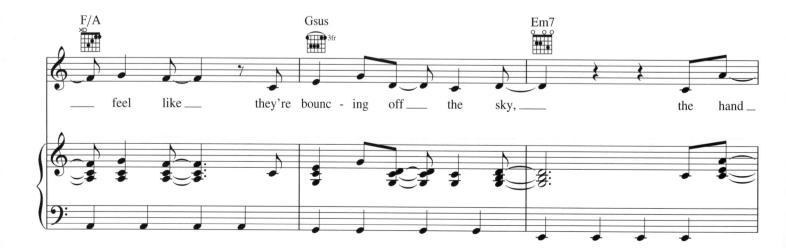

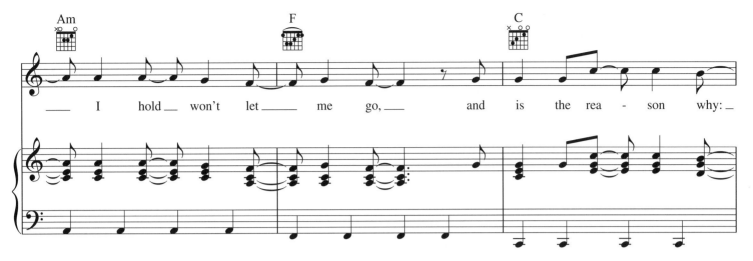

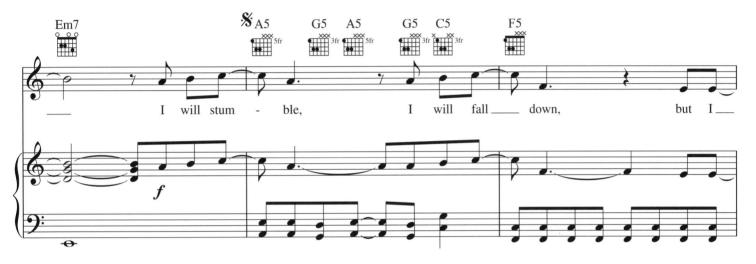

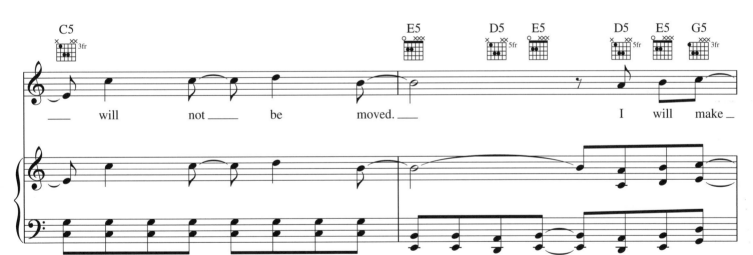

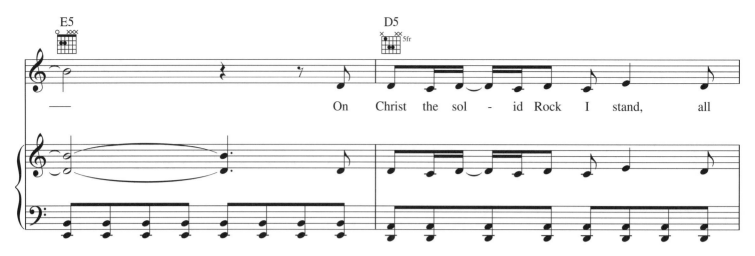

On Christ the sol - id Rock I stand, all

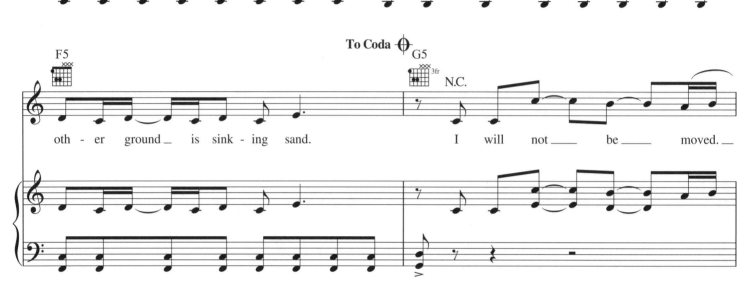

oth - er ground is sink - ing sand. I will not be moved.

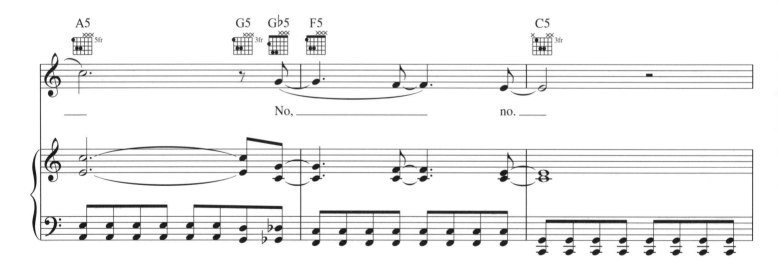

No, no.

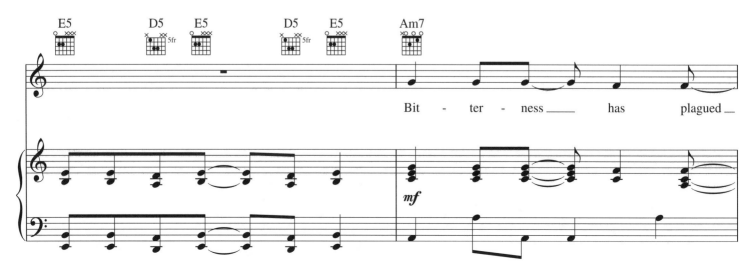

Bit - ter - ness has plagued

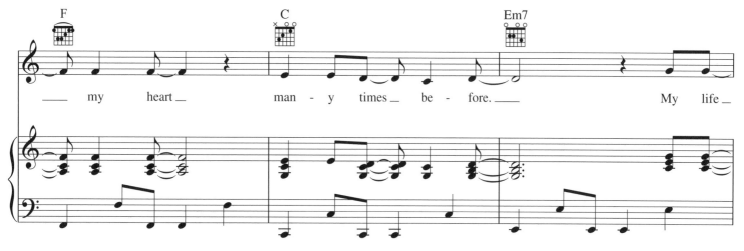

my heart ___ man - y times ___ be - fore. ___ My life ___

has been ___ like bro - ken glass, ___ and I have kept ___ the score ___

of all ___ my shat - tered dreams. ___ And though ___ it seemed ___ that

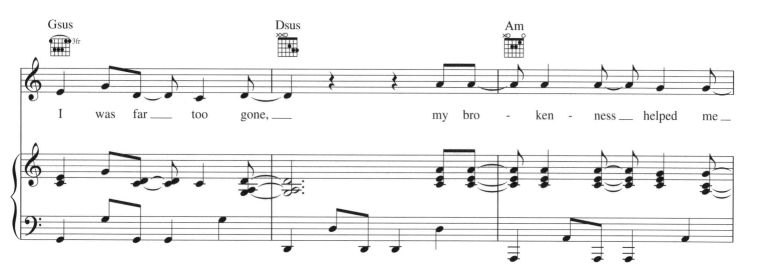

I was far ___ too gone, ___ my bro - ken - ness ___ helped me ___

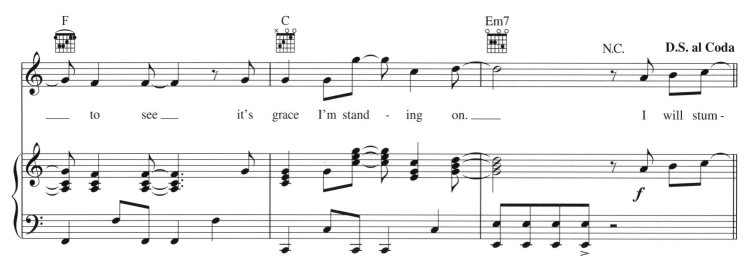

_to see ___ it's grace I'm stand - ing on. ___ I will stum-_

_I will not ___ be ___ moved. ___ And the cha - os in ___ my life ____

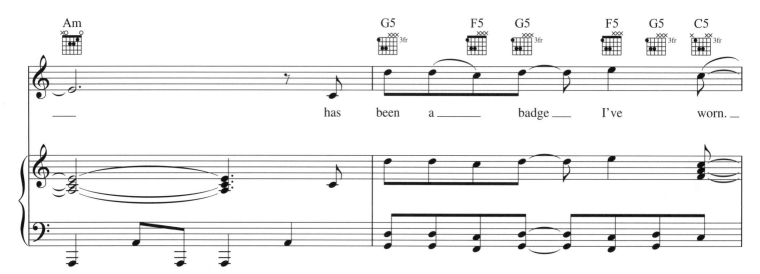

_has been a ____ badge ___ I've ____ worn. ____

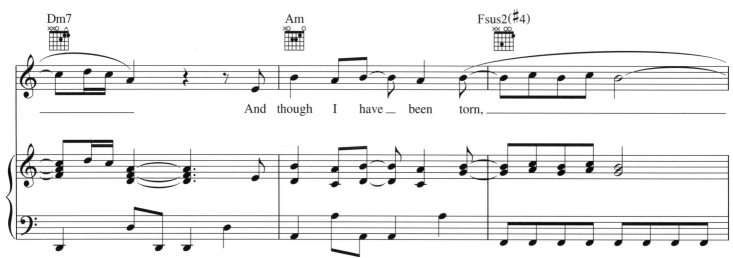

_____ And though I have ___ been torn, _____

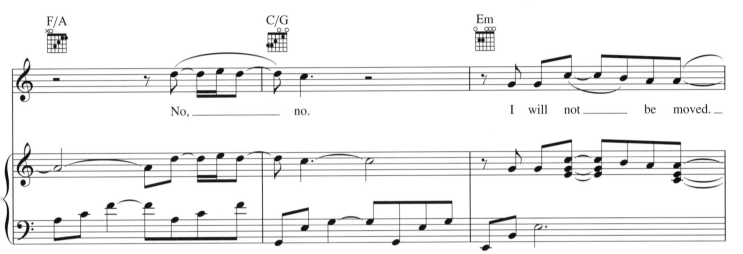

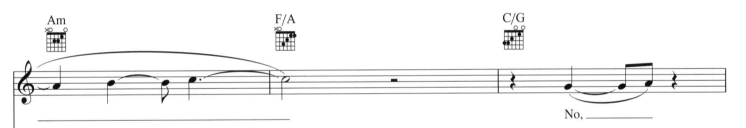

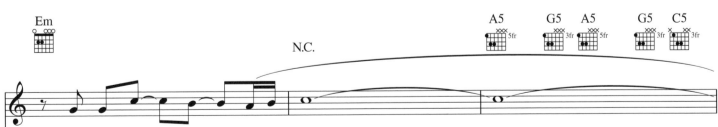

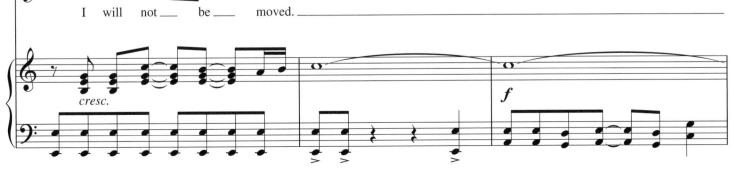

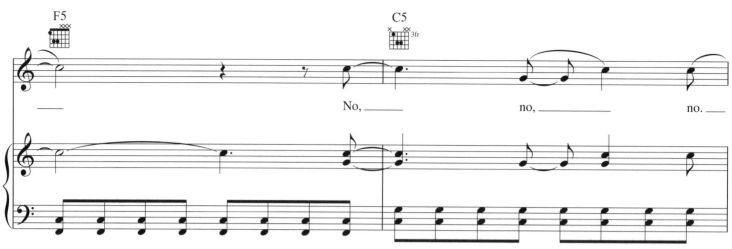

No, _____ no, _____ no. _____

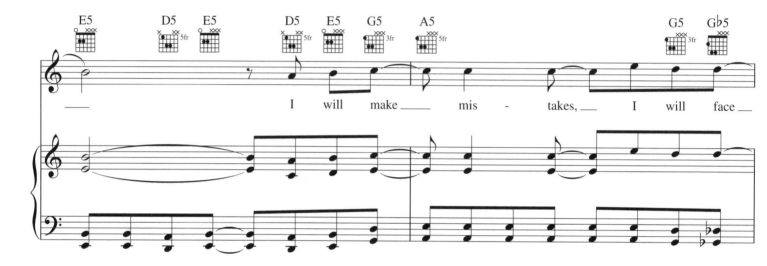

_____ I will make _____ mis - takes, _____ I will face

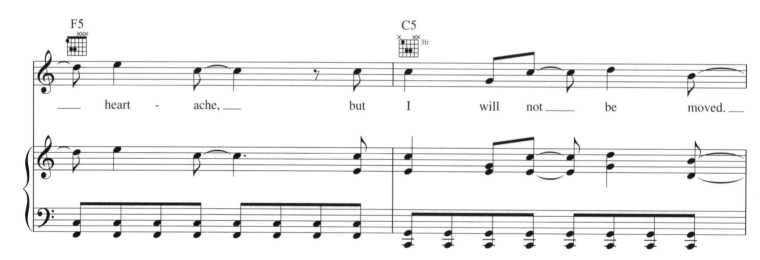

_____ heart - ache, _____ but I will not _____ be moved.

_____ On Christ the sol - id Rock I stand, all

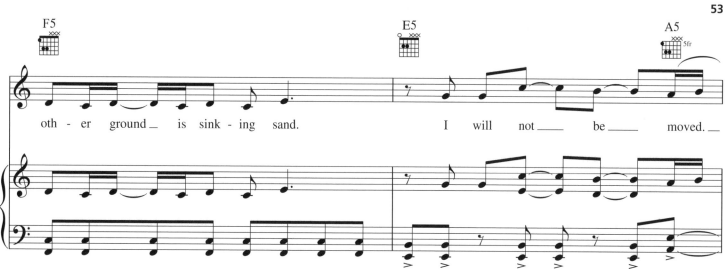

oth - er ground __ is sink - ing sand. I will not ___ be ___ moved. __

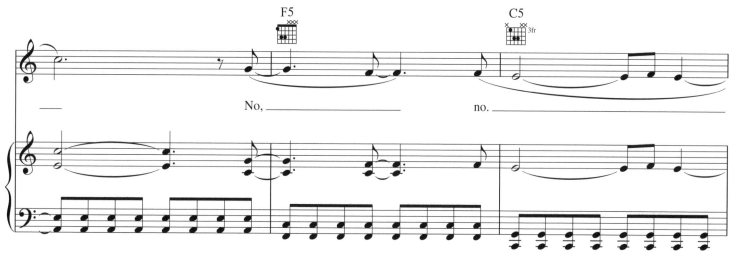

No, _____ no. _____

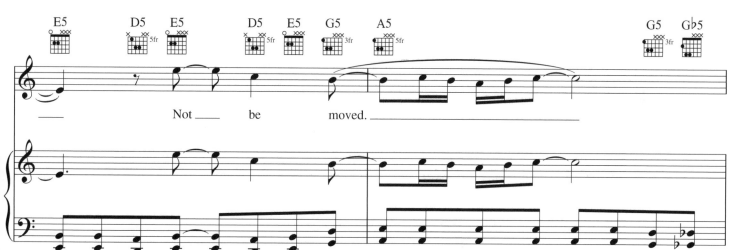

Not ___ be moved. _____

No, ___ no, ___ no, no, ___ no.

IN BETTER HANDS

Words and Music by CATHY LEE GRAVITT,
JIM DADDARIO and THOM HARDWELL

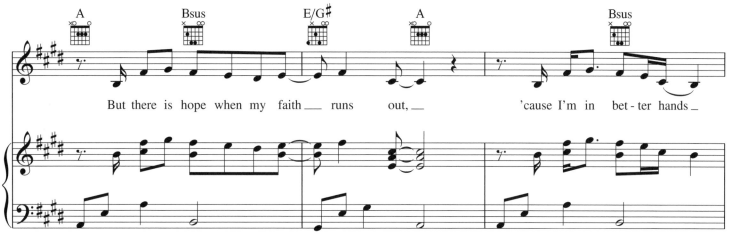

But there is hope when my faith____ runs out,____ 'cause I'm in bet - ter hands____

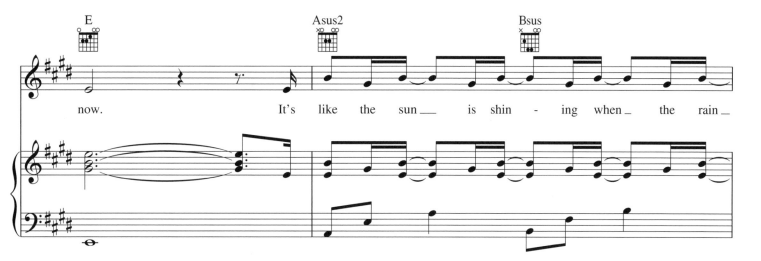

now. It's like the sun____ is shin - ing when____ the rain____

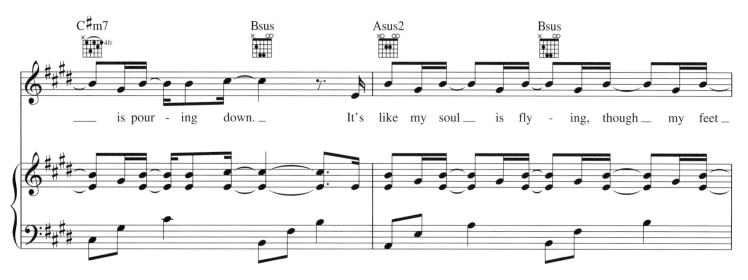

____ is pour - ing down.____ It's like my soul____ is fly - ing, though____ my feet____

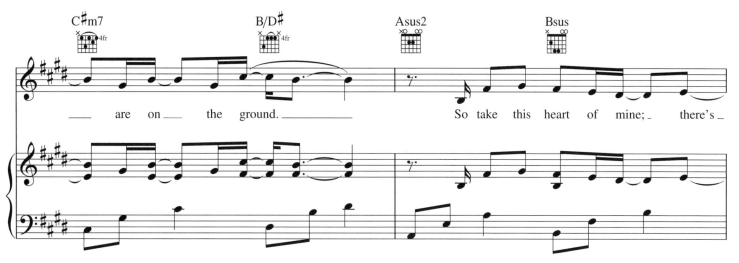

____ are on____ the ground._____ So take this heart of mine;____ there's____

no doubt __ I'm in bet-ter hands __ now. I am

strong __ all be-cause __ of You. __ I stand in awe of ev-'ry moun-

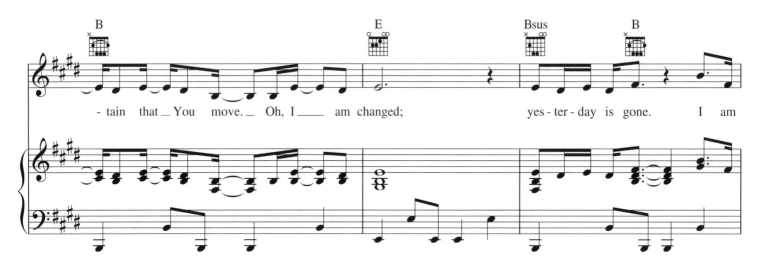

-tain that __ You move. __ Oh, I __ am changed; yes-ter-day is gone. I am

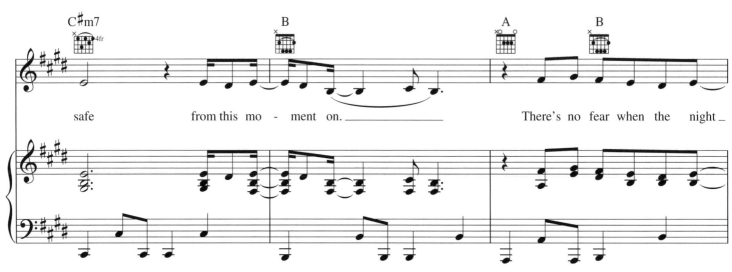

safe from this mo-ment on. __ There's no fear when the night __

____ comes 'round. _____ I'm in bet-ter hands __ now. _____ It's_

_like the sun __ is shin - ing when __ the rain ___ is pour - ing down. __ It's_

_like my soul __ is fly - ing, though __ my feet ___ are on __ the ground. _____

_So take this heart of mine; __ there's __ no doubt __ I'm in bet - ter hands _____

_____ now. _____ It's

like the sun ___ is shin - ing when __ the rain ___ is pour - ing down. __ It's

like my soul __ is fly - ing, though __ my feet ___ are on __ the ground. ___ It's

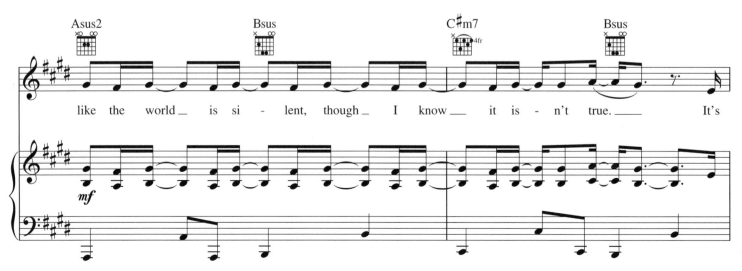

like the world __ is si - lent, though __ I know __ it is - n't true. ____ It's

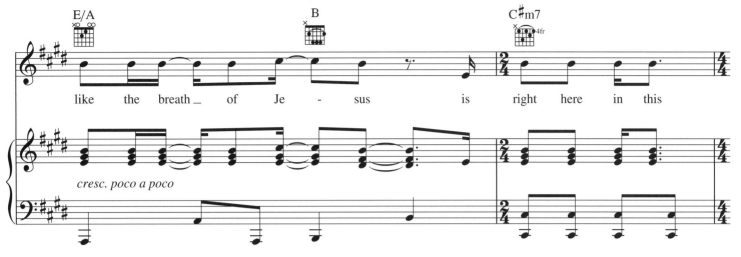

like the breath __ of Je - sus is right here in this

room. __ So take this heart of mine; __ there's __ no doubt __

I'm in bet - ter hands __ now. __ I'm in bet - ter hands __

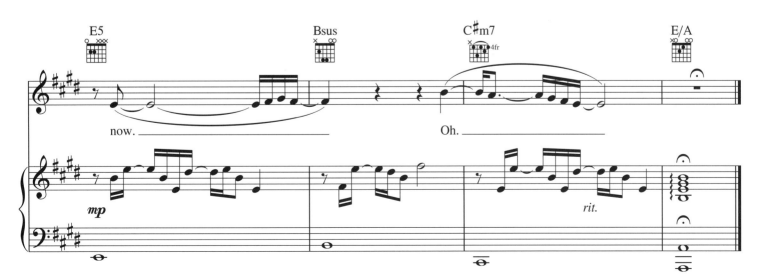

now. __ Oh. __

LIVE FOR TODAY

Words and Music by
NATALIE GRANT

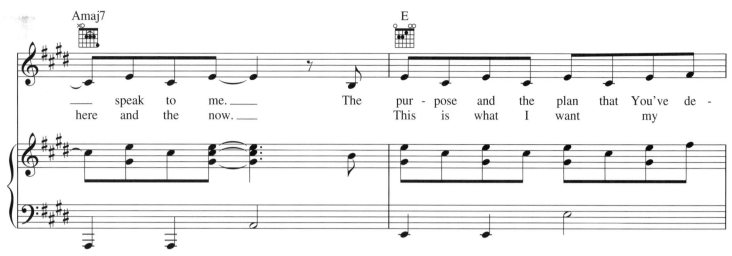

speak to me. ___ The pur - pose and the plan that You've de -
here and the now. ___ This is what I want my

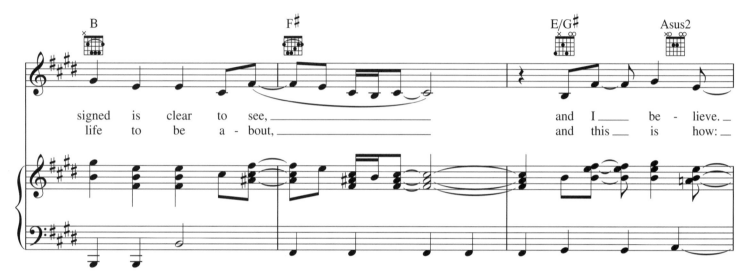

signed is clear to see, _____ and I ___ be - lieve. ___
life to be a - bout, _____ and this ___ is how: ___

___ I'm gon - na live ___ for to - day. ___ I'm gon - na fol -

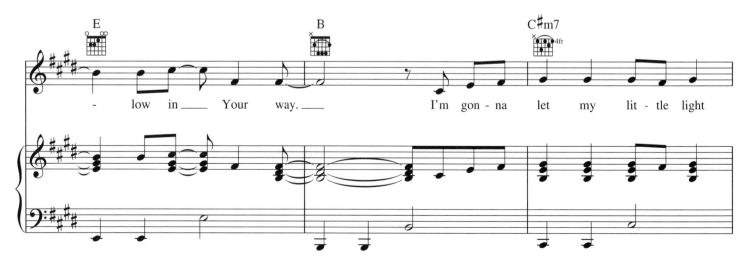

- low in ___ Your way. ___ I'm gon - na let my lit - tle light

live it for __ to-day. __ Yeah, __ oh. __ My oh, so cra-

-zy life __ has got me spin-ning 'round _

__ and 'round, _ hang-ing up-side __ down, __ tak-ing

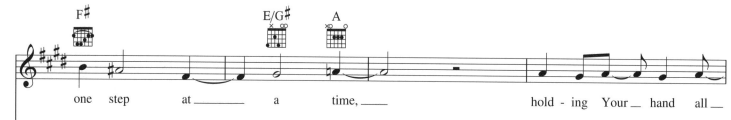

one step at __ a time, __ hold-ing Your __ hand all __

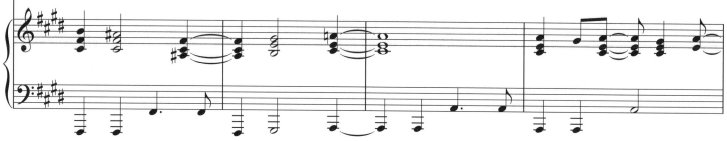

the way, __ and it 'll be o - kay, yeah, __ yeah. I

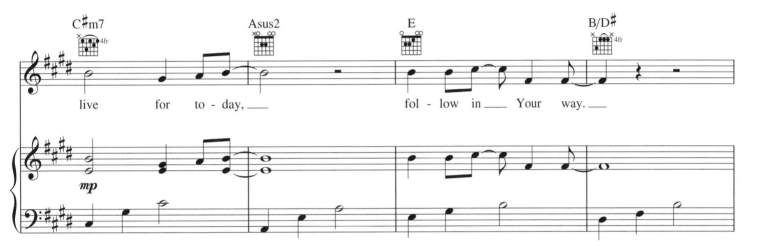

live for to - day, __ fol - low in __ Your way. __

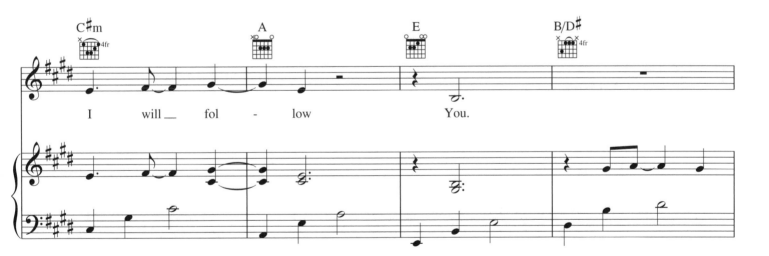

I will __ fol - low You.

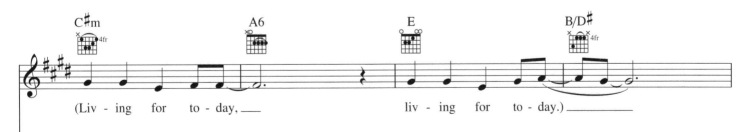

(Liv - ing for to - day, __ liv - ing for to - day.) __

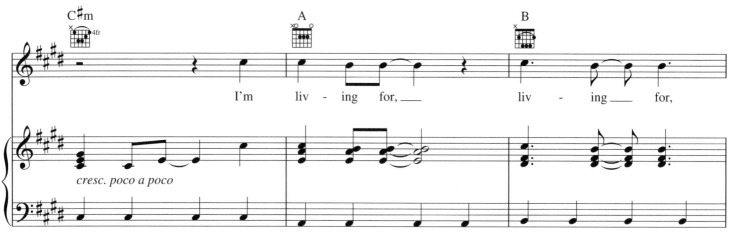

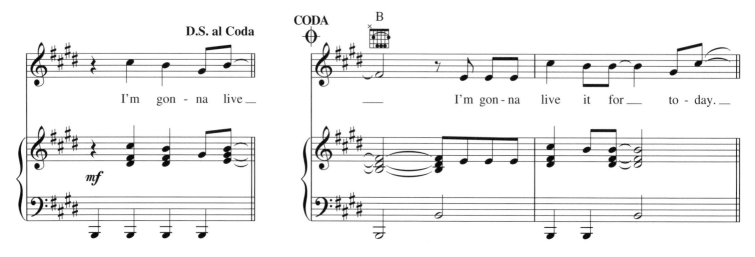

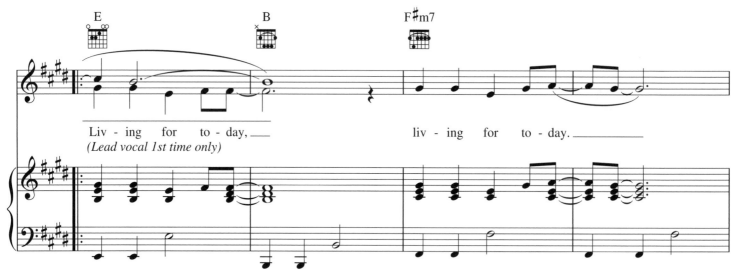

THE REAL ME

Words and Music by
NATALIE GRANT

With reflection

Foolish heart, ___ looks like we're here a-gain.

Same old game of plas-tic smile, ___ don't let an-y-bod-y in, ___

hid-ing my ___ heart-ache. ___ Will this glass ___ house

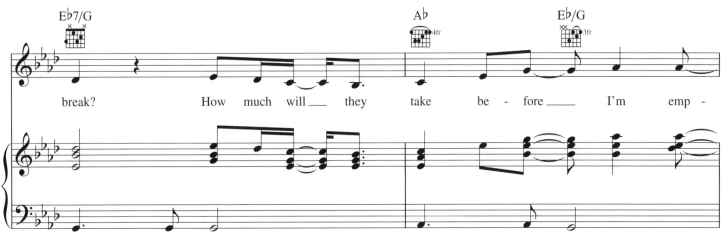

break? How much will ___ they take be - fore ___ I'm emp -

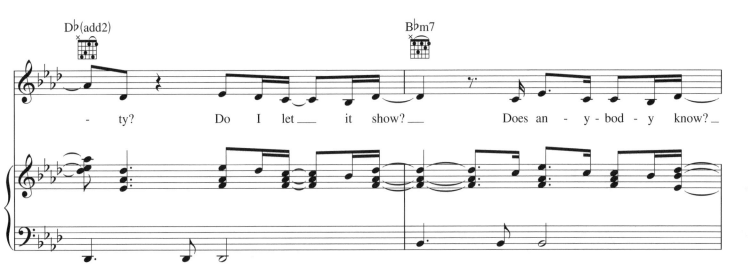

- ty? Do I let ___ it show? ___ Does an - y - bod - y know? ___

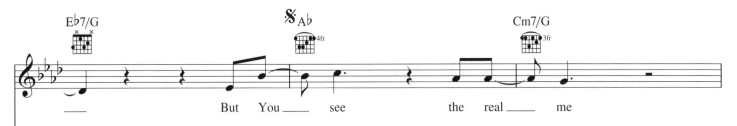

___ But You ___ see the real ___ me

rall. *mf* *a tempo*

hid - ing in ___ my skin, bro - ken from with - in. ___ Un - veil ___ me com - plete -

-ly. I'm loos-en-ing ___ my grasp. There's ___ no need to mask ___ my frail-

To Coda ⊕

-ty, 'cause You ___ see the real ___ me. ___

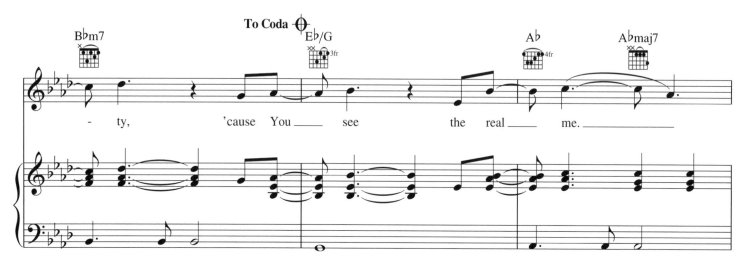

Paint-ed on, ___ life is be-hind a mask. ___ Self-in-flict-ed

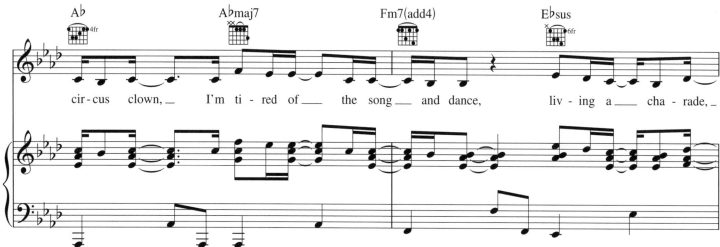

cir-cus clown, ___ I'm ti-red of ___ the song ___ and dance, liv-ing a ___ cha-rade, ___

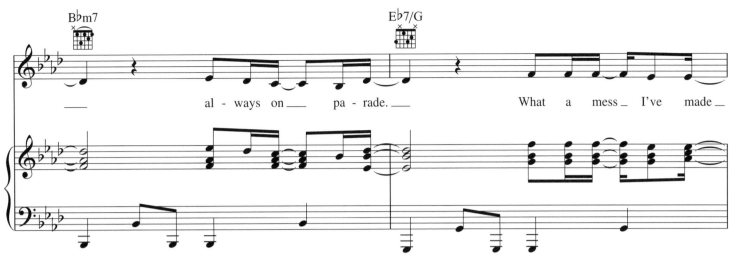

al - ways on___ pa - rade.___ What a mess___ I've made___

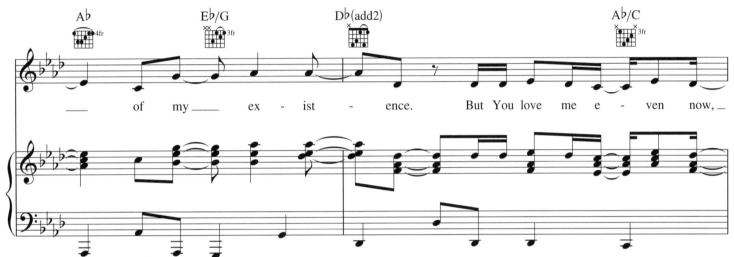

___ of my___ ex - ist - ence. But You love me e - ven now,___

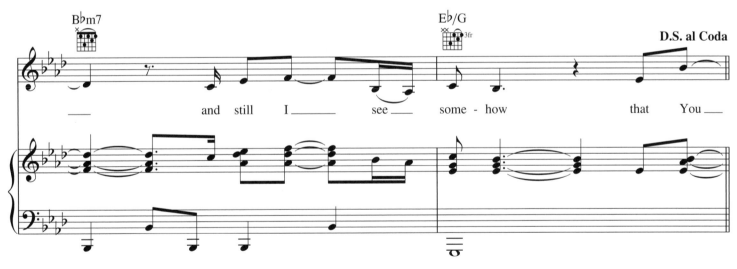

___ and still I___ see___ some - how that You___

___ see _____ the real ___ me. ___

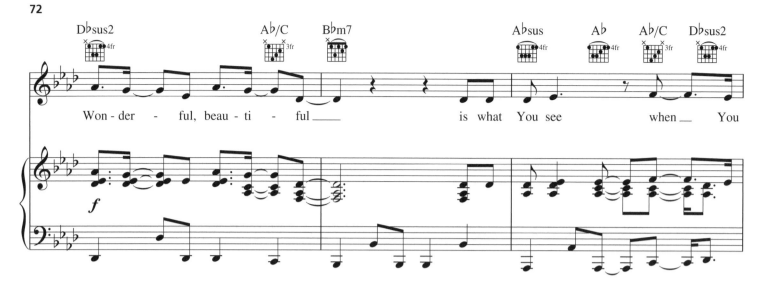

Won - der - ful, beau - ti - ful ___ is what You see when ___ You

look at me. ___ You're turn - ing ___ the tat - tered ___ fab - ric of ___ my

life ___ in - to ___ a per - fect tap - es - try. ___

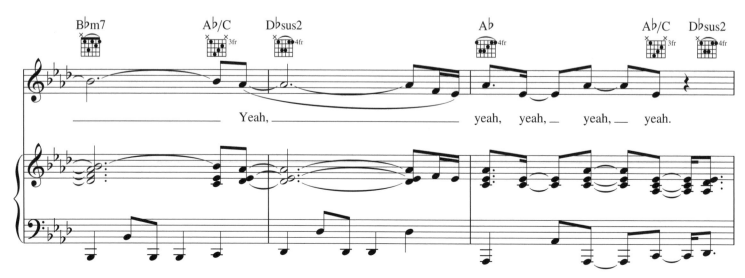

_____ Yeah, _____ yeah, yeah, ___ yeah, ___ yeah.

Oh, I just wan-na __ be me, _____ yeah, yeah, yeah, _ yeah. __ I

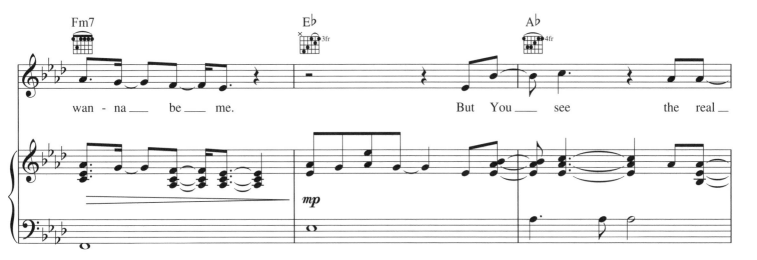

wan-na __ be __ me. But You __ see the real __

__ me, yeah, __ hid-ing in __ my skin, bro-ken from with-in. __ Un-veil __

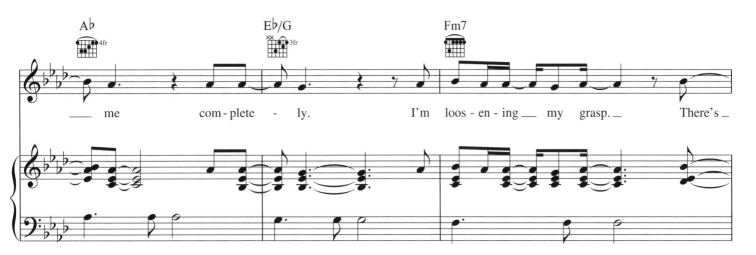

__ me com-plete-ly. I'm loos-en-ing __ my grasp. __ There's _

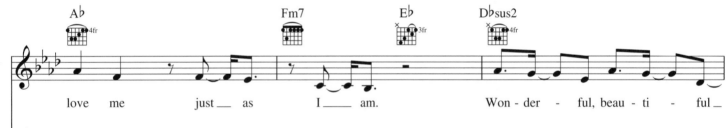

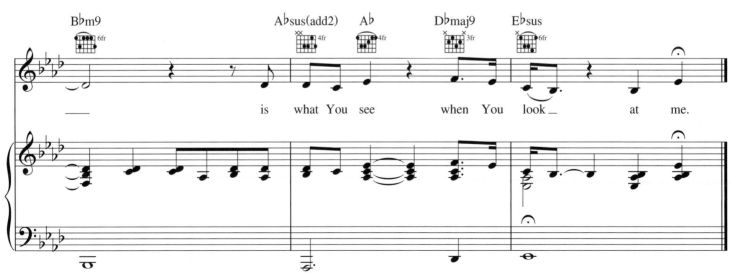

WHENEVER YOU NEED SOMEBODY

Words and Music by NATALIE GRANT,
JAMES COLLINS, KEVIN STOKES
and BERNIE HERMS

walk down the road. Re - mem - ber, you're nev - er a -

lone. When - ev - er you need some - bod - y, when - ev - er you

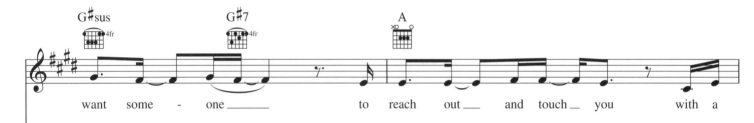

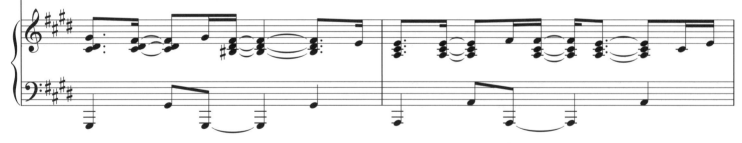

want some - one to reach out and touch you with a

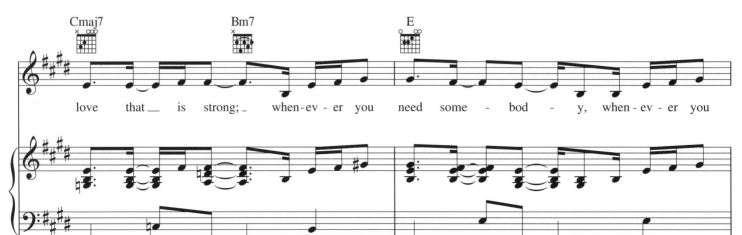

love that is strong; when - ev - er you need some - bod - y, when - ev - er you

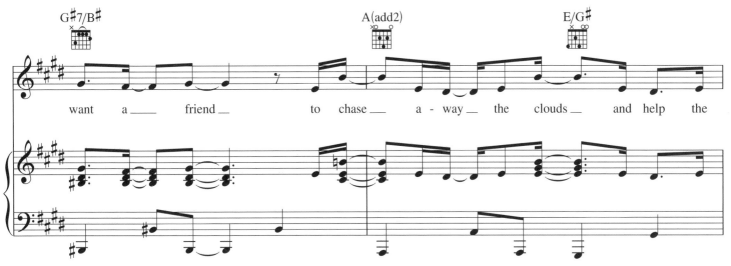

want a ___ friend ___ to chase ___ a - way ___ the clouds ___ and help the

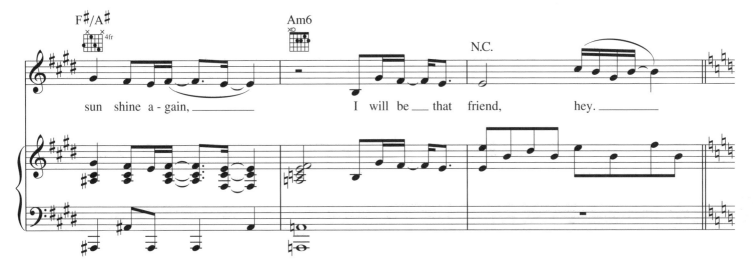

sun shine a - gain, _____ I will be ___ that friend, hey. _____

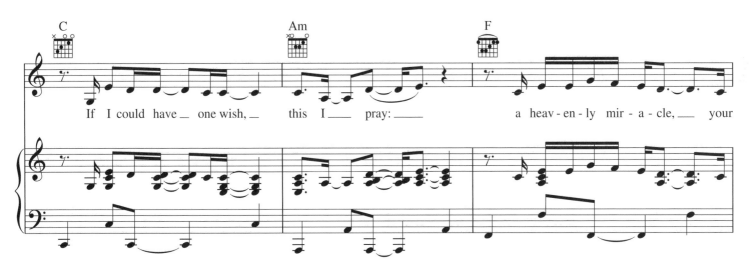

If I could have ___ one wish, ___ this I ___ pray: ___ a heav - en - ly mir - a - cle, ___ your

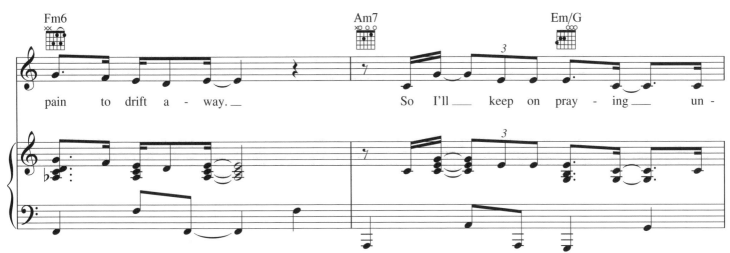

pain to drift a - way. ___ So I'll ___ keep on pray - ing ___ un -

til that __ day comes. __ Re - mem - ber __ that I'll _____ be the one. __

_____ When - ev - er you need some - bod - y, when - ev - er you

want some - one _____ to reach out __ and touch __ you with a

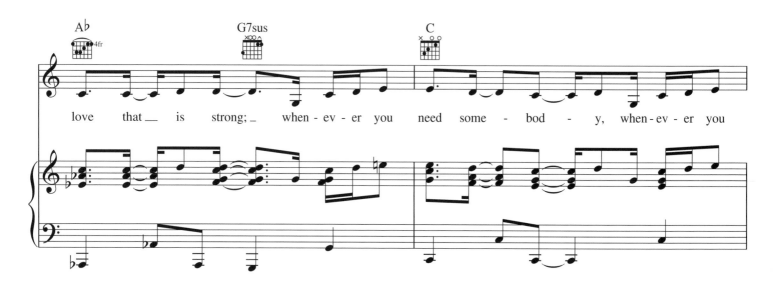

love that __ is strong; __ when - ev - er you need some - bod - y, when - ev - er you

want a ___ friend ___ to chase a - way ___ the clouds ___ and help the sun ___

___ shine a - gain, _____ I will be ___ that friend. ___

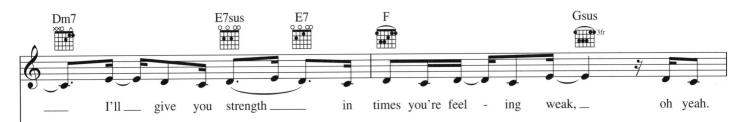

___ I'll ___ give you strength _____ in times you're feel - ing weak, ___ oh yeah.

I'll give you hope and help ___ you to be - lieve, yeah. _____ When - ev - er you

need some - bod - y, when - ev - er you want some - one ____ to

reach out ____ and touch ____ you with a love that ____ is strong; ____ when - ev - er you

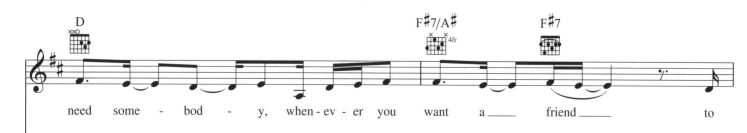

need some - bod - y, when - ev - er you want a ____ friend ____ to

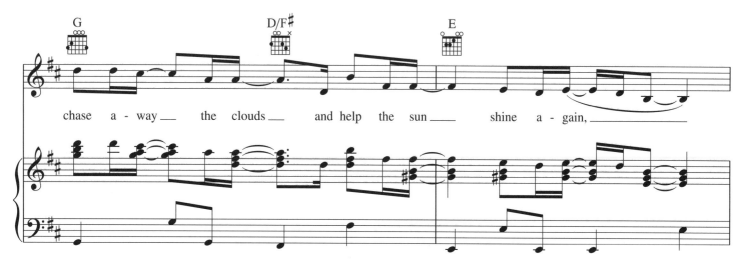

chase a - way ____ the clouds ____ and help the sun ____ shine a - gain, ____

THERE IS A GOD

Words and Music by NATHAN DiGESARE,
NATALIE GRANT and BRUCE SUDANO

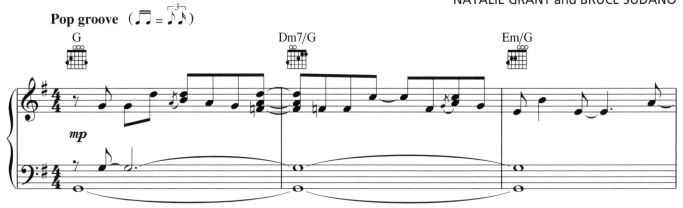

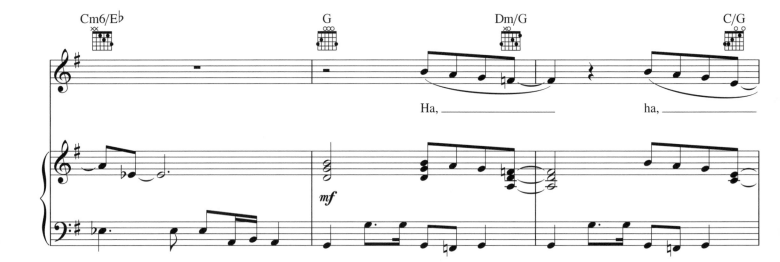

Ha, _____ ha, _____

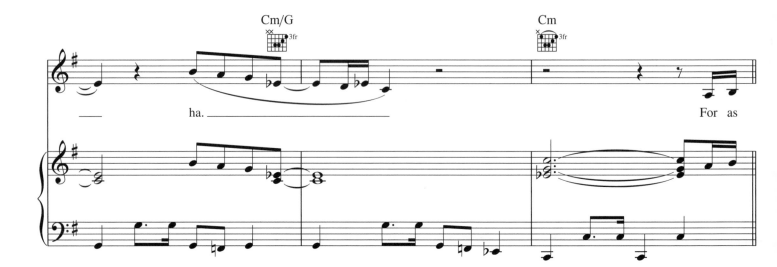

— ha. _____ For as

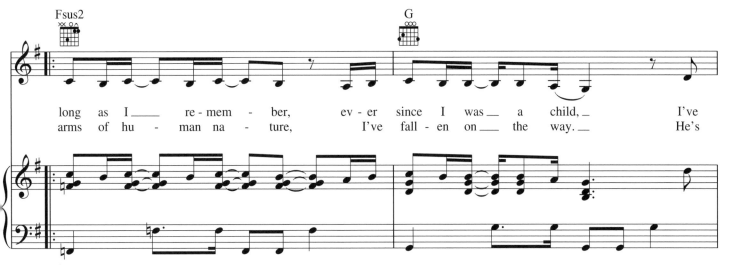

long as I ____ re-mem - ber, ev - er since I was ___ a child, ___ I've
arms of hu - man na - ture, I've fall - en on ___ the way. ___ He's

had the un - der - stand - ing in _____ my ___ heart that
heard the des - per - a - tion of _____ my ___ cry. One

there is a ____ Cre - a - tor, a Mas - ter of ___ de - sign who
drink of liv - ing wa - ter can heal the hurt ___ in - side. He

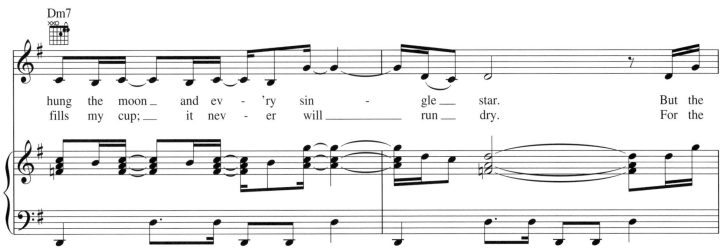

hung the moon ___ and ev - 'ry sin - gle ___ star. But the
fills my cup; ___ it nev - er will _____ run ___ dry. For the

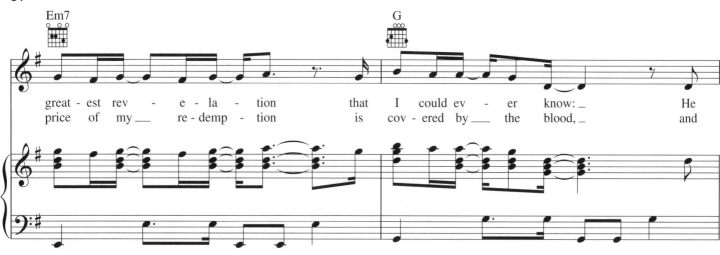

great-est rev - e - la - tion that I could ev - er know: ___ He
price of my ___ re - demp - tion is cov - ered by ___ the blood, ___ and

loves me in my weak - ness and calls ___ me His ___ own. ___
I have been made wor - thy by His ___ gift of ___ love. ___

I have a hope ___ and I be - lieve. ___ My faith is a - live, ___

___ my spir - it is free. ___ Though He's un - seen, ___ still I know deep ___

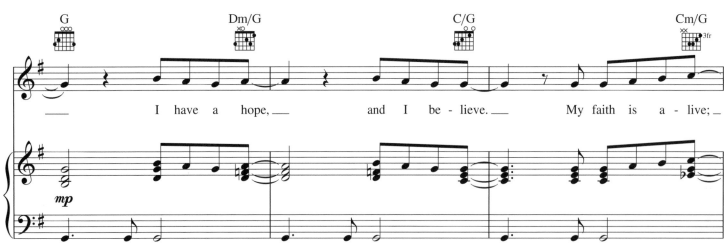

I have a hope, ___ and I be - lieve. ___ My faith is a - live; ___

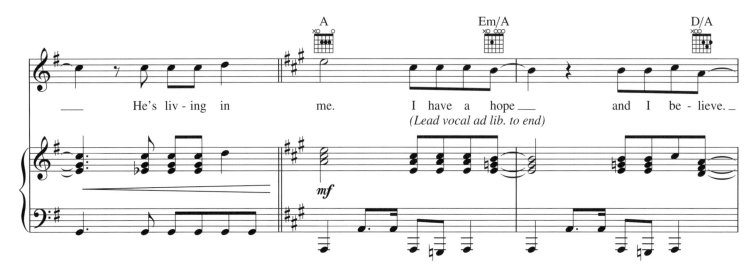

He's liv - ing in me. I have a hope ___ and I be - lieve. ___

(Lead vocal ad lib. to end)

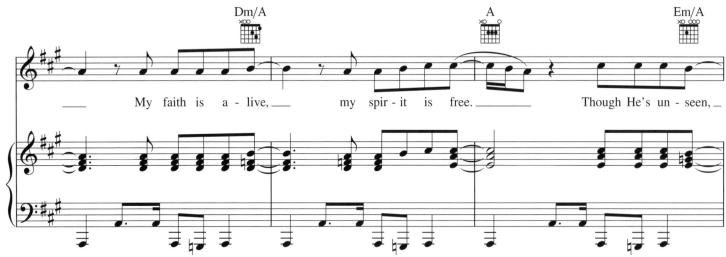

My faith is a - live, ___ my spir - it is free. ___ Though He's un - seen, ___

still I know deep ___ with - in ___ my soul ___ there is ___ a God. ___

I have a hope ___ and I be - lieve. ___ My faith is a - live, ___

___ my spir - it is free. ___ Though He's un - seen, ___

___ still I know deep ___ with - in ___ my soul ___

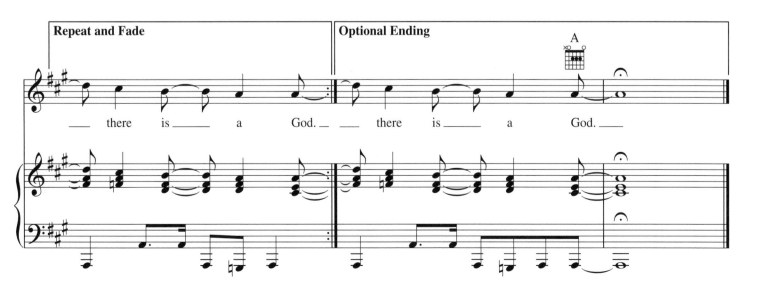

Repeat and Fade

Optional Ending

___ there is ___ a God. ___ there is ___ a God. ___

WAITING FOR A PRAYER

Words and Music by NATALIE GRANT,
WENDY A. WILLS and BERNIE HERMS

Steady Disco beat

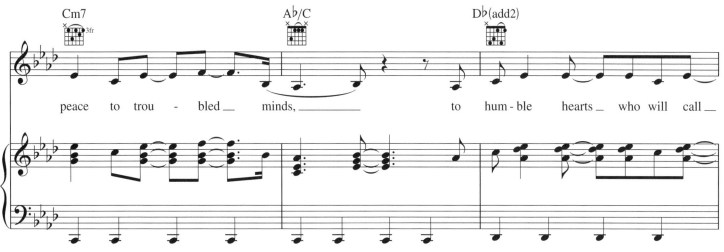

peace to trou - bled ___ minds, _____ to hum - ble hearts ___ who will call ___

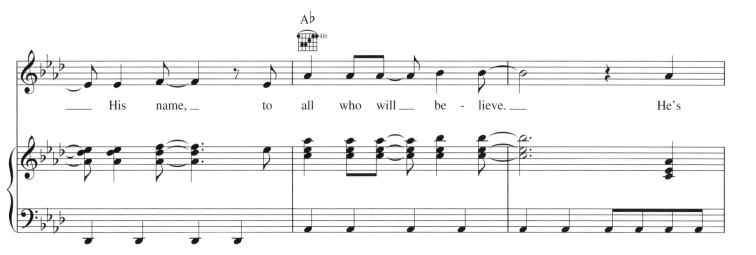

___ His name, ___ to all who will ___ be - lieve. ___ He's

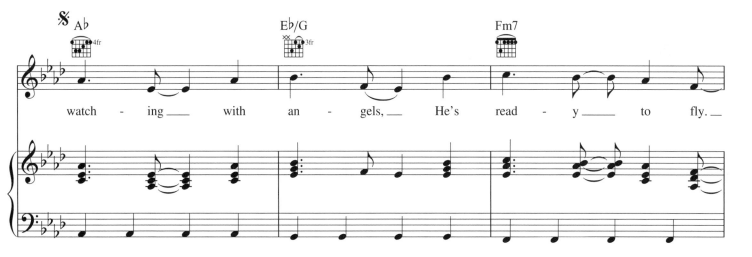

watch - ing ___ with an - gels, ___ He's read - y ___ to fly. ___

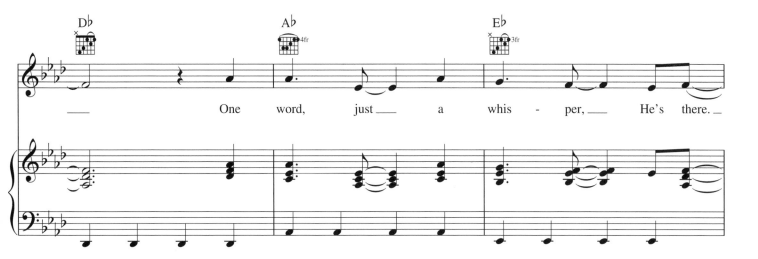

___ One word, just ___ a whis - per, ___ He's there. ___

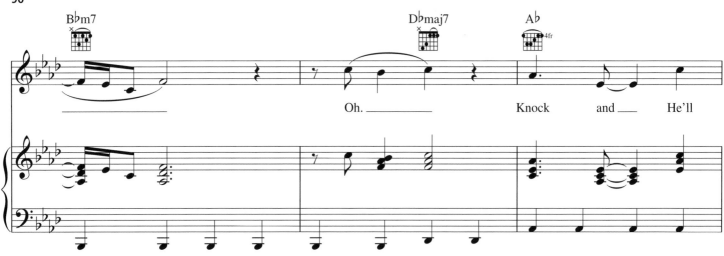

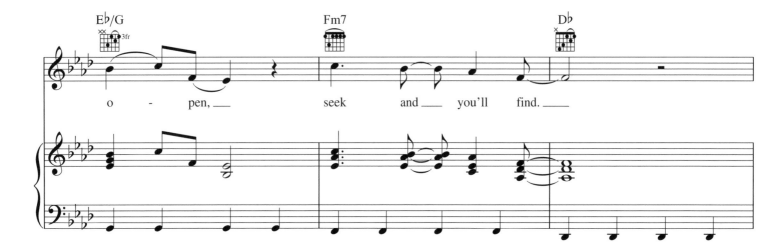

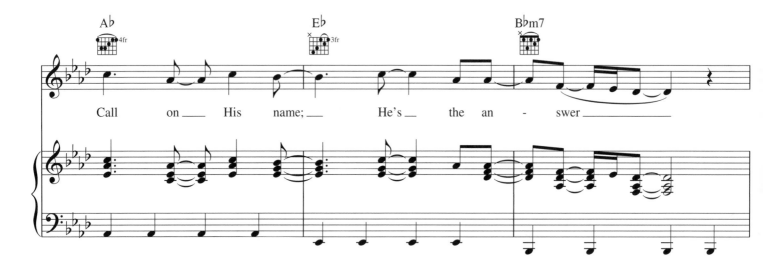

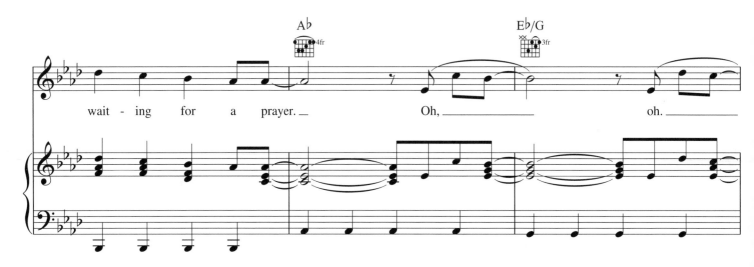

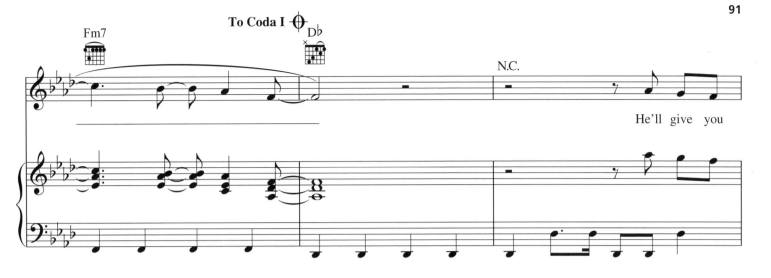

To Coda I

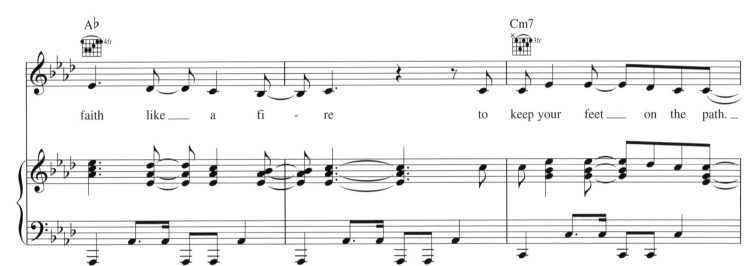

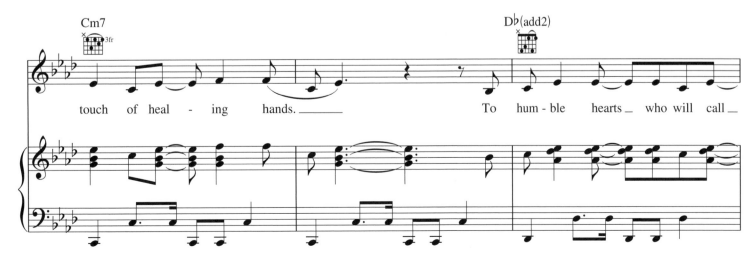

His name, __ to all who will __ be - lieve, _____ He's

D.S. al Coda I

CODA I

__ Fall on __ your knees __ and __ be - lieve __

__ the Fa - ther hears __ you when __ you pray, __ an - y - time, __

__ night __ or day. __ And He __ will say, _____

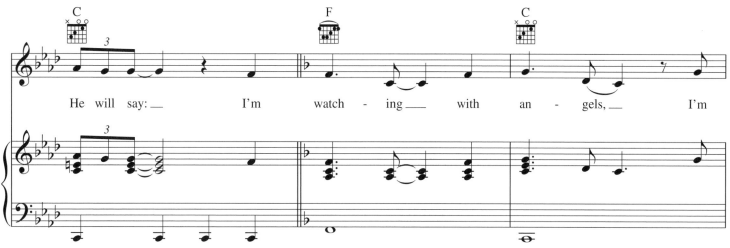

He will say: __ I'm watch - ing __ with an - gels, __ I'm

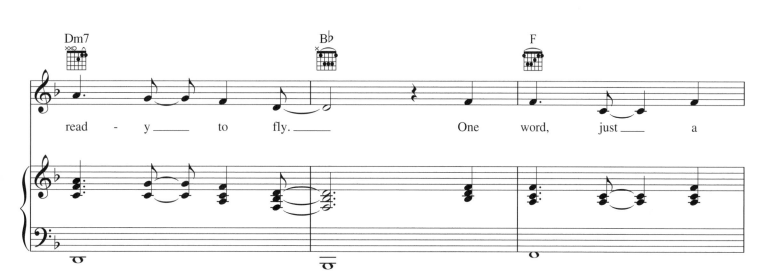

read - y __ to fly. __ One word, just __ a

whis - per, __ I'll __ be there. __

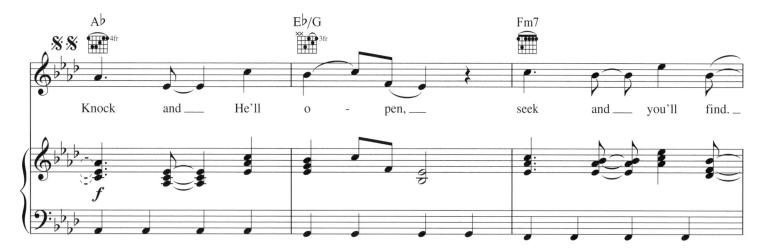

Knock and __ He'll o - pen, __ seek and __ you'll find. __

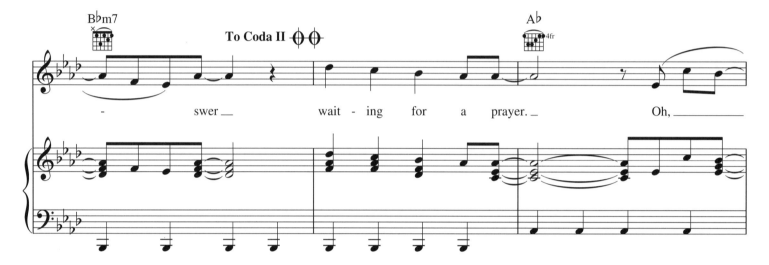

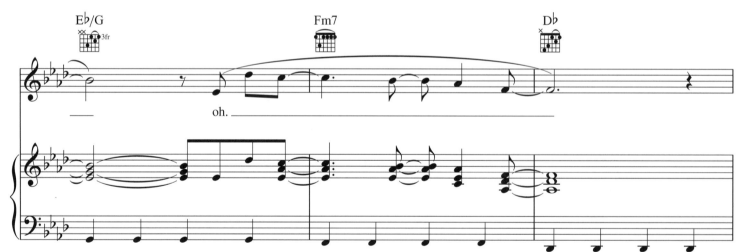

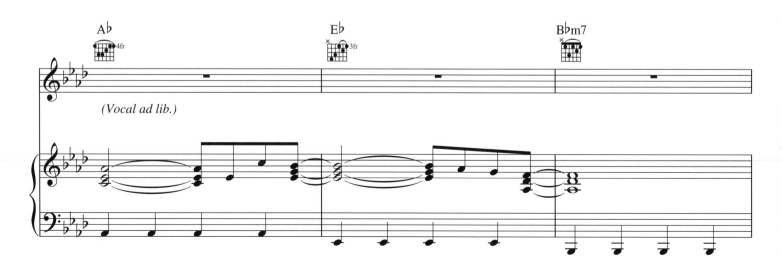

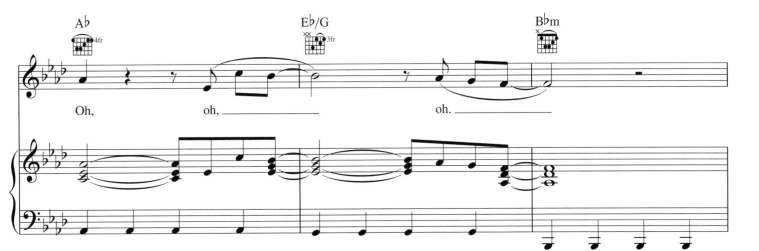

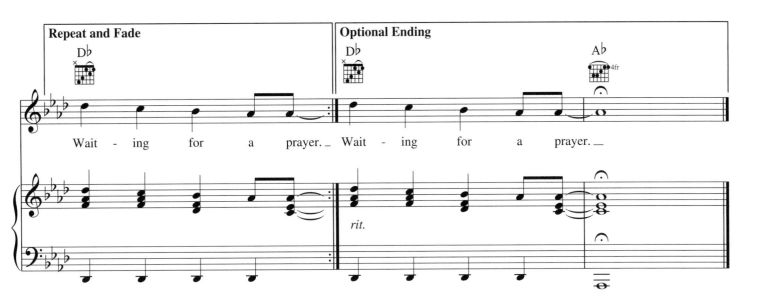

WHAT ARE YOU WAITING FOR

Words and Music by BRIDGET BENENATE,
STEVE BOOKER and MATTHEW GERRARD

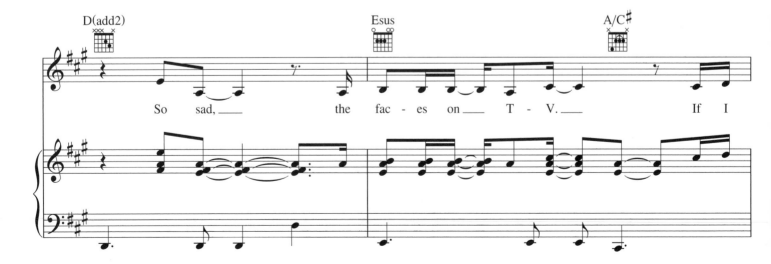

tried to make a dif - f'rence, would it help an - y - way? ___ But

then I stop, ___ and to my - self ___ I say: ___ So you wan - na change ___ the world? ___

___ What are you wait - ing for? ___ You say you're gon - na start ___ right now. ___

___ What are you wait - ing for? ___ It on - ly takes ___ one voice, ___ so

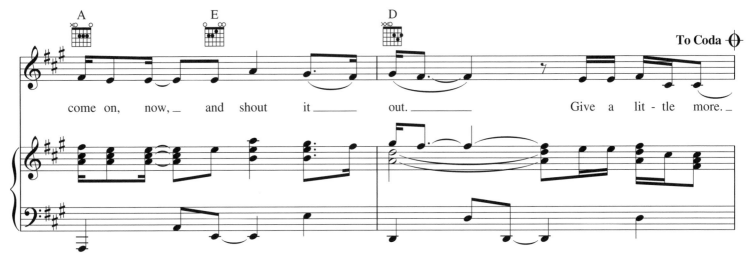

come on, now, __ and shout it _____ out. _____ Give a lit - tle more. __

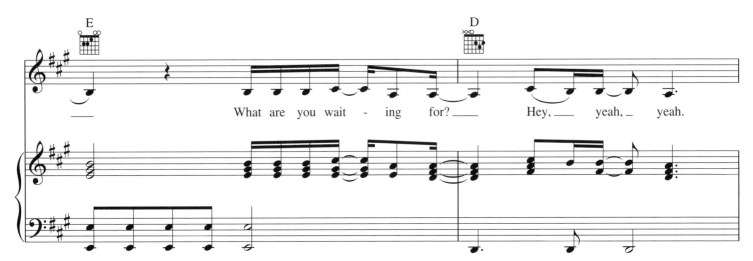

What are you wait - ing for? ____ Hey, ____ yeah, __ yeah.

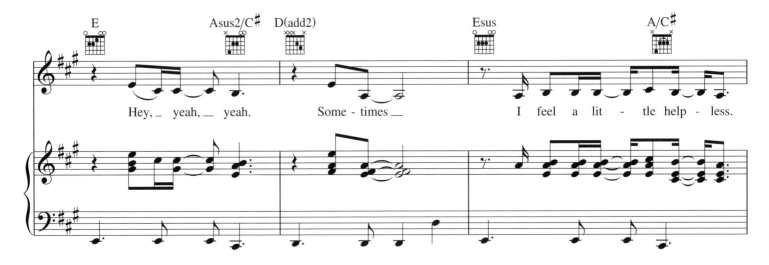

Hey, __ yeah, __ yeah.   Some - times __   I feel a lit - tle help - less.

Seems like __   I can't do a thing. __   But an - y - thing __ is pos - si - ble; __

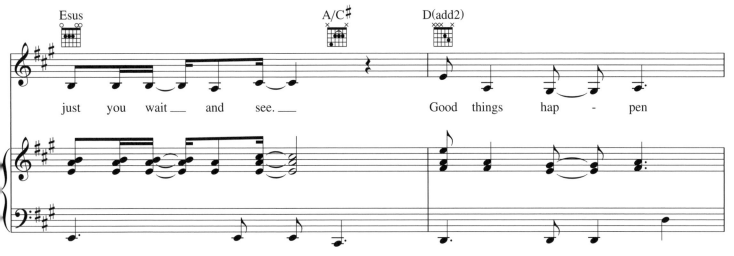

just you wait___ and see.___ Good things hap - pen

if___ you just_____ be - lieve.___ So you wan - na change___ the world?___

D.S. al Coda

CODA

___ What are you wait - ing for?___ Some - day, some - how,___ you're gon - na

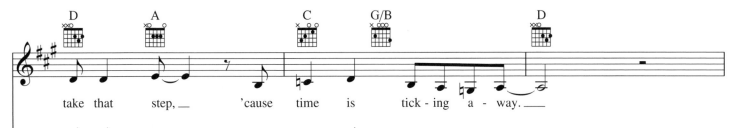

take that step,___ 'cause time is tick - ing a - way.___

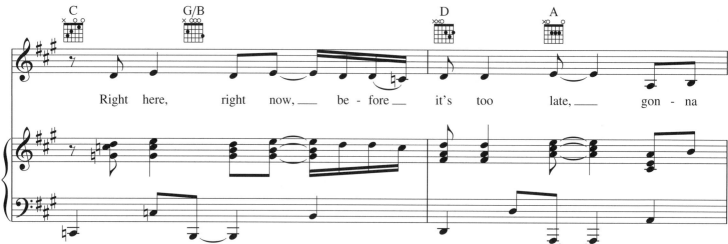

Right here, right now, ___ be-fore ___ it's too late, ___ gon-na

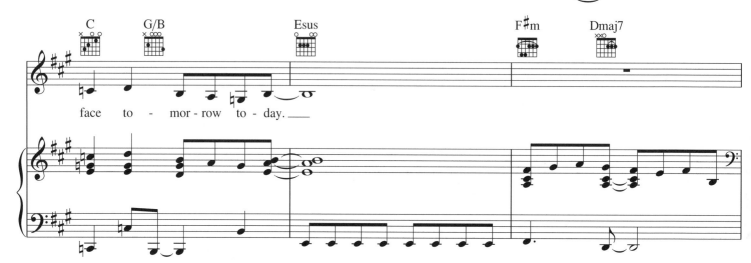

face to - mor - row to - day. ___

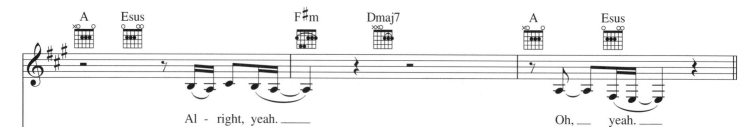

Al - right, yeah. ___   Oh, ___ yeah. ___

___ So you wan - na change ___ the world? ___   What are you wait - ing for? ___

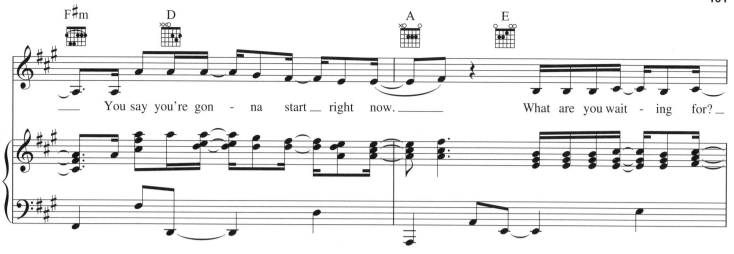

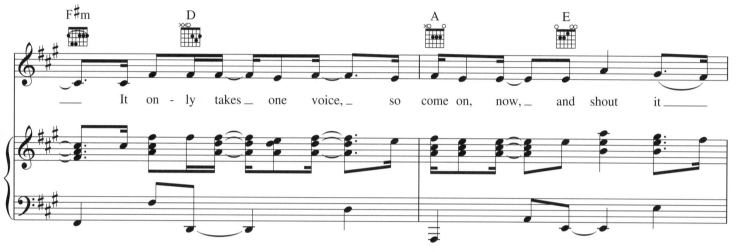

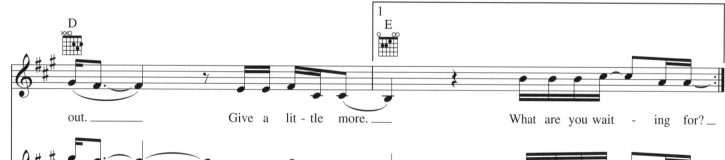

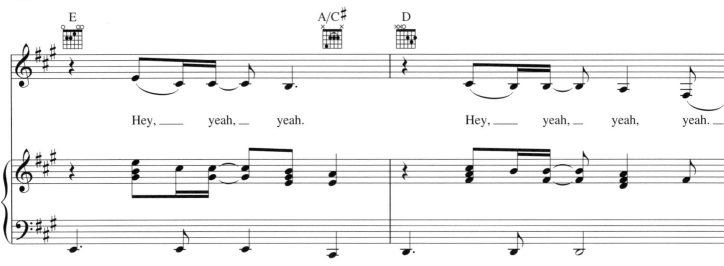

Hey, ___ yeah, ___ yeah.   Hey, ___ yeah, ___ yeah, ___ yeah.

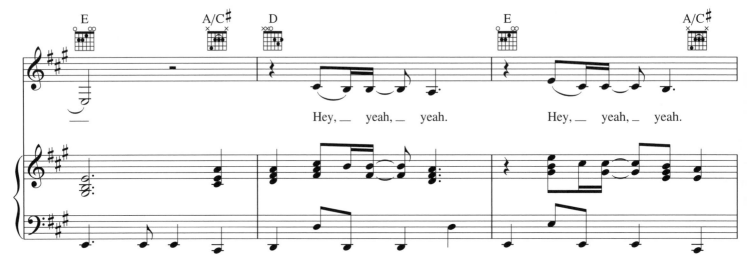

Hey, ___ yeah, ___ yeah.   Hey, ___ yeah, ___ yeah.

Hey, ___ yeah, ___ yeah, yeah. ___   What are you wait - ing for?

What are you wait - ing for?

More Contemporary Christian Folios from Hal Leonard
Arranged for Piano, Voice and Guitar

AVALON – THE GREATEST HITS
This best-of collection showcases 15 signature songs from throughout their career, plus a brand new tune soon to be fan favorite, the radio hit "Still My God." Includes: Adonai • Can't Live a Day • New Day • You Were There • and more.
00307056 P/V/G.......................................$17.99

JEREMY CAMP – SPEAKING LOUDER THAN BEFORE
Our matching folio to the latest from this three-time ASCAP Songwriter of the Year includes the hit "There Will Be a Day" and 11 more: Capture Me • I'm Alive • My Fortress • Surrender • You Will Be There • and more.
00307031 P/V/G.......................................$16.99

CASTING CROWNS – UNTIL THE WHOLE WORLD HEARS
Matching folio to the 2009 release featuring 11 songs from this Christian pop group: Always Enough • Joyful, Joyful • At Your Feet • Holy One • To Know You • Mercy • Blessed Redeemer • and more.
00307107 P/V/G.......................................$16.99

STEVEN CURTIS CHAPMAN – BEAUTY WILL RISE
Matching folio to Chapman's touching release that was written in response to the death of one of his daughters. 12 songs, including: Just Have to Wait • Faithful • Heaven Is the Face • I Will Trust You • and more.
00307100 P/V/G.......................................$16.99

DAVID CROWDER*BAND – CHURCH MUSIC
Our matching folio to the innovative 2009 release features 17 tunes, including the hit single "How He Loves" and: All Around Me • Can I Lie Here • Oh, Happiness • Shadows • We Are Loved • What a Miracle • and more.
00307089 P/V/G.......................................$17.99

AMY GRANT – GREATEST HITS
This collection assembles 19 of her finest, including: Angels • Baby Baby • El Shaddai • Father's Eyes • Good for Me • Lead Me On • Simple Things • Stay for Awhile • and more.
00306948 P/V/G $17.95

HEATHER HEADLEY – AUDIENCE OF ONE
Features 10 songs or medleys of well-known gospel standards plus some Headley originals and other recent favorites: Here I Am to Worship • I Know the Lord Will Make a Way • Simply Redeemed • Zion • and more.
00307057 Piano/Vocal....................$16.99

KUTLESS – IT IS WELL
Matching folio to the second worship album from these Christian rockers, featuring 12 songs, including: Give Us Clean Hands • God of Wonders • Redeemer • What Faith Can Do • and more.
00307099 P/V/G $16.99

MARY MARY – THE SOUND
Features vocal arrangements with piano accompaniment for all 11 songs off the Gospel chart-topping 5th CD from this R&B/gospel duo. Includes the Grammy-winning single "Get Up" and: Boom • Dirt • Forgiven Me • God in Me • I Worship You • and more.
00307039 Piano/Vocal....................$16.99

RECOLLECTION: THE BEST OF NICHOLE NORDEMAN
This 17-song collection features the finest releases from this popular CCM singer/songwriter, plus two new songs – "Sunrise" and "Finally Free." Includes: Brave • Fool for You • Real to Me • River God • This Mystery • and more.
00306633 P/V/G.......................................$17.95

PHILLIPS, CRAIG & DEAN – THE ULTIMATE COLLECTION
31 songs spanning the career of this popular CCM trio: Favorite Song of All • Hallelujah (Your Love Is Amazing) • I Want to Be Just like You • Shine on Us • Your Grace Still Amazes Me • and more.
00306789 P/V/G.......................................$19.95

THE BEST OF MATT REDMAN
14 modern worship songs, including: Beautiful News • Better Is One Day • Blessed Be Your Name • The Heart of Worship • Once Again • Shine • Undignified • You Never Let Go • and more.
00307080 P/V/G.......................................$16.99

SANCTUS REAL – WE NEED EACH OTHER
The fourth CD from this Dove Award-winning Toledo quintet features 10 songs: Half Our Lives • Leap of Faith • Legacy • Sing • Turn On the Lights • We Need Each Other • Whatever You're Doing (Something Heavenly) • and more.
00306976 P/V/G.......................................$16.95

SWITCHFOOT – THE BEST YET
This greatest hits compilation features the newly released song "This Is Home" and 17 other top songs. Includes: Concrete Girl • Dare You to Move • Learning to Breathe • Meant to Live • Only Hope • Stars • and more.
00307030 P/V/G $17.99

THIRD DAY – REVELATION
All 13 songs from the chart-topping album, including the #1 single "Call My Name" and: Born Again • I Will Always Be True • Let Me Love You • Run to You • Slow Down • Take It All • and more.
00307005 P/V/G.......................................$16.95

THE CHRIS TOMLIN COLLECTION
15 songs from one of the leading artists and composers in contemporary worship music, including the favorites: Amazing Grace (My Chains Are Gone) • Indescribable • We Fall Down • and more.
00306951 P/V/G.......................................$16.95

THE BEST OF CECE WINANS
14 favorite songs from the gospel superstar: Alabaster Box • He's Always There • It Wasn't Easy • Looking Back at You • Pray • Purified • Throne Room • What About You • and more.
00306912 P/V/G.......................................$16.99

FOR MORE INFORMATION, SEE YOUR LOCAL MUSIC DEALER, OR WRITE TO:

HAL•LEONARD® CORPORATION
7777 W. BLUEMOUND RD. P.O. BOX 13819 MILWAUKEE, WI 53213

For a complete listing of the products we have available, visit us online at www.halleonard.com

Prices, contents, and availability subject to change without notice.

THE BEST OF CONTEMPORARY CHRISTIAN MUSIC

The ancient Greek "sign of the fish" (Ichthys) is an instantly recognizable Christian symbol in pop culture. It is used on car bumpers, clothing, jewelry, business logos, and more. Hal Leonard is proud to offer The Fish Series, showcasing the wide variety of music styles that comprise the Contemporary Christian genre. From the early pioneers of CCM to today's biggest hits, there's something for everyone!

CHRISTMAS (Green Book)
40 Contemporary Christian holiday favorites, including: Christmas Angels • Christmas Is All in the Heart • He Made a Way in a Manger • Joseph's Lullaby • Manger Throne • Not That Far from Bethlehem • 2000 Decembers Ago • While You Were Sleeping • and more.
00311755 P/V/G.................................$19.95

EARLY YEARS (Orange Book)
41 songs, including: The Day He Wore My Crown • Father's Eyes • I Wish We'd All Been Ready • Love Crucified Arose • Rise Again • Sing Your Praise to the Lord • Who Will Save the Children • Your Love Broke Through • and more.
00311756 P/V/G.................................$19.99

INSPIRATIONAL (Blue Book)
42 songs of encouragement and exaltation, including: Call on Jesus • Find Your Wings • God Will Make a Way • Healing Rain • Jesus Will Still Be There • On My Knees • Say the Name • Your Grace Still Amazes Me • and many more.
00311757 P/V/G.................................$19.95

POP (Red Book)
44 top pop hits from favorite Contemporary Christian artists, including: Always Have, Always Will • Brave • Circle of Friends • For Future Generations • If We Are the Body • Simple Things • To Ever Live Without Me • What It Means • and more.
00311758 P/V/G.................................$21.95

PRAISE (Yellow Book)
50 songs of praise and worship, including: Agnus Dei • Before the Throne of God Above • Come Just As You Are • He Knows My Name • Majesty • Open Our Eyes • Worthy of Worship • You Are My All in All • and many more.
00311759 P/V/G.................................$19.99

ROCK (Black Book)
41 rock hits from some of the biggest names in Contemporary Christian music, including: All Around Me • Count Me In • Everlasting God • I'm Not Alright • Meant to Live • No Matter What It Takes • Tunnel • Undo • and more.
00311760 P/V/G.................................$19.95

WEDDING (White Book)
40 songs from Contemporary Christian artists for the bride and groom's big day, including: Cinderella • God Knew That I Needed You • Household of Faith • I Will Be Here • Look What Love Has Done • A Page Is Turned • This Day • Without Love • and more.
00311761 P/V/G.................................$19.99

WORSHIP (Purple Book)
50 songs perfect for a worship band or solo praise, including: Amazing Grace (My Chains Are Gone) • Beautiful One • Days of Elijah • Forever • In Christ Alone • Mighty to Save • Revelation Song • Sing to the King • and many more.
00311762 P/V/G.................................$21.95

HAL•LEONARD® CORPORATION

7777 W. BLUEMOUND RD. P.O. BOX 13819 MILWAUKEE, WI 53213

Visit Hal Leonard Online at
www.halleonard.com

0109